All Together Now

D1318155

JARED BERNSTEIN

All Together Now

Common Sense for a Fair Economy

BK

BERRETT-KOEHLER PUBLISHERS, INC.
San Francisco
a BK Currents book

Copyright © 2006 by Jared Bernstein

All rights reserved. No part of this publication may be reproduced, distributed, or transmitted in any form or by any means, including photocopying, recording, or other electronic or mechanical methods, without the prior written permission of the publisher, except in the case of brief quotations embodied in critical reviews and certain other noncommercial uses permitted by copyright law. For permission requests, write to the publisher, addressed "Attention: Permissions Coordinator," at the address below.

Berrett-Koehler Publishers, Inc.
235 Montgomery Street, Suite 650
San Francisco, CA 94104-2916
Tel: (415) 288-0260 Fax: (415) 362-2512   www.bkconnection.com

ORDERING INFORMATION

Quantity sales. Special discounts are available on quantity purchases by corporations, associations, and others. For details, contact the "Special Sales Department" at the Berrett-Koehler address above.

Individual sales. Berrett-Koehler publications are available through most bookstores. They can also be ordered direct from Berrett-Koehler:
Tel: (800) 929-2929; Fax: (802) 864-7626; www.bkconnection.com

Orders for college textbook/course adoption use. Please contact Berrett-Koehler:
Tel: (800) 929-2929; Fax: (802) 864-7626.

Orders by U.S. trade bookstores and wholesalers. Please contact Publishers Group West, 1700 Fourth Street, Berkeley, CA 94710.
Tel: (510) 528-1444; Fax (510) 528-3444.

Berrett-Koehler and the BK logo are registered trademarks of Berrett-Koehler Publishers, Inc.

Printed in the United States of America

Berrett-Koehler books are printed on long-lasting acid-free paper. When it is available, we choose paper that has been manufactured by environmentally responsible processes. These may include using trees grown in sustainable forests, incorporating recycled paper, minimizing chlorine in bleaching, or recycling the energy produced at the paper mill.

LIBRARY OF CONGRESS CATALOGING-IN-PUBLICATION DATA

Bernstein, Jared.
    All together now : common sense for a fair economy / by Jared Bernstein
        p. cm.
    Includes bibliographical references and index.
    1. United States–Economic policy–2001- 2. United States–Social policy–
1993- 3. Capitalism–United States. 4. Individualism–United States. I. Title.

HC106.83.B47 2006
330.973–dc22
                                                                    2005057116

ISBN-10: 1-57675-387-5; ISBN-13: 978-1-57675-387-3

First Edition

11 10 09 08 07 06   10 9 8 7 6 5 4 3 2 1

Design and production by Seventeenth Street Studios

TO KATE
whose quiet company in the early mornings was comforting and inspiring.

CONTENTS

Acknowledgments   ix

INTRODUCTION

Ready or Not, You're on Your Own   3

CHAPTER ONE

Risk Shifting, from Coolidge to Katrina   13

CHAPTER TWO

The Economist behind the Curtain   37

CHAPTER THREE

The "All Together Now" Plan   60

CHAPTER FOUR

How to Talk to a YOYO   95

CONCLUSION

It Takes a Movement   117

APPENDIX

Do YOYO Policies Yield Better Economic Outcomes?   131

Index   145
About the Author   155

ACKNOWLEDGMENTS

Many people helped this project come to fruition, but none more than Johanna Vondeling from Berrett-Koehler Publishers. It was she who sent me an e-mail out of the blue suggesting that perhaps there was a book in some of the articles I had been writing for *The American Prospect* (so thanks to Bob Kuttner and his colleagues over there too). She's worked with me every step of the way, and her encouragement, enthusiasm, and ear for what works have been invaluable to me. They say that a good editor makes you believe in her, but a great editor makes you believe in yourself. She's great.

The rest of the staff at B-K has been extremely helpful as well. Special mention to Jeevan Sivasubramaniam for all he's done to help move the book along. Karen Seriguchi's copyediting made the text much more readable.

My colleagues at the Economic Policy Institute continue to educate me, and I'm fortunate to work with such smart, progressive people. Larry Mishel has been an intellectual touchstone and a close friend since the day we met almost fifteen years (and seven books) ago. Sylvia Allegretto, another great colleague and coauthor, and Elise Gould (my health care guru) also deserve mention, as do Josh Bivens, Nancy Coleman, Ross Eisenbrey, Michael Ettlinger, David Kusnet, Lee Price, and Max Sawicky. Yulia Fungard is, simply put, one of the world's greatest research assistants. Debra Agostini provided friendly and efficient help with administrative matters.

Two reviewers, Charlie Derber and Mark Engler, provided extremely useful guidance; their input helped improve the quality of the text. Brad Coley, Debbie Cowden, Mark Greenberg, Mitchell Max, and Joel Rogers also made helpful suggestions along the way.

Finally, I could never have carved out the time to write this were it not for my wife, Kay Arndorfer. I benefit from her love and friendship every day.

In the following pages I offer nothing more than simple facts, plain arguments, and common sense.

— THOMAS PAINE

Ready or Not, You're on Your Own

I ONCE HEARD an allegory about mealtime in heaven and hell. It turns out that in both places, meals are served at a huge round table with lots of delicious food in the center. The food is out of reach, but everyone's got really long forks.

In hell, everyone starves because, while people can reach the food with their forks, the forks are much longer than their arms, so nobody can turn a fork around and eat what's on the end of it.

In heaven, faced with the same problem, people eat well. How? By feeding each other.

Protecting the rights of individuals has always been a core American value. Yet in recent years the emphasis on individualism has been pushed to the point where, like the diners in hell, we're starving. This political and social philosophy is hurting our nation, endangering our future and that of our children, and, paradoxically, making it harder for individuals to get a fair shot at the American dream.

This extreme individualism dominates the way we talk about the most important aspects of our economic lives, those that reside in the intersection of our living standards, our government, and the future opportunities for ourselves and our children. The message, sometimes implicit but often explicit, is, *You're on your own*. Its acronym, YOYO, provides a useful shorthand to summarize this destructive approach to governing.

The concept of YOYO, as used in this book, isn't all that complicated. It's the prevailing vision of how our country should be governed. As such, it embodies a set of values, and at the core of the YOYO value system is hyper-individualism: the notion that whatever the challenges we face as a nation, the best way to solve them is for people to fend for themselves. Over the past few decades, this harmful vision has generated a set of policies with that hyper-individualistic gene throughout their DNA.

The YOYO crowd—the politicians, lobbyists, and economists actively promoting this vision—has stepped up its efforts to advance its policies in recent years, but hyper-individualism is not a new phenomenon. Chapter 1 documents archaeological evidence of YOYO thinking and policies from the early 1900s, along with their fingerprint: a sharp increase in the inequality of income, wealth, and opportunity. The most recent incarnation can be found in the ideas generated by the administration of George W. Bush, but the YOYO infrastructure—the personnel with a vested interest in the continued dominance of these policies—will not leave the building with Bush. Unless, that is, we recognize the damage being done and make some major changes.

One central goal of the YOYO movement is to continue and even accelerate the trend toward shifting economic risks from the government and the nation's corporations onto individuals and their families. You can see this intention beneath the surface of almost every recent conservative initiative: Social Security privatization, personal accounts for health care (the so-called Health Savings Accounts), attacks on labor market regulations, and the perpetual crusade to slash the government's revenue through regressive tax cuts—a strategy explicitly tagged as "starving the beast"—and block the government from playing a useful role in our economic lives. You can even see this go-it-alone principle in our stance toward our supposed international allies.

While this fast-moving reassignment of economic risk would be bad news in any period, it's particularly harmful today. As the new century unfolds, we face prodigious economic challenges, many of which have helped to generate both greater inequalities and a higher degree of economic insecurity in our lives. But the dominant vision has failed to develop a hopeful, positive narrative about how these challenges can be met in such a way as to uplift the majority.

Instead, messages such as "It's your money" (the mantra of the first George W. Bush campaign in 2000), and frames such as "the ownership society," stress an ever shrinking role for government and much more individual risk taking. Yet global competition, rising health costs, longer life spans with weaker pensions, less secure employment, and unprecedented inequalities of opportunity and wealth are calling for a much broader, more inclusive approach to helping all of us meet these challenges, one that taps government as well as market solutions.

To cite one potent example, 46 million people lack health coverage, and the share of our economy devoted to health care is headed for unsustainable levels. We urgently need to begin planning a viable alternative, such as a system of universal coverage as exists in every other advanced economy. In every case, these countries insure their citizens, control health costs better than we do, and have better overall health outcomes. Yet our leaders want to solve the problem with an individualistic, market-based system of private accounts designed to cut costs by shifting risk from the insurer to the patient, unleashing more of the very market forces that got us into this mess in the first place.

As I stress throughout, those crafting such policies are trapped in the YOYO paradigm, one where common-sense solutions, even those embraced by the rest of the advanced world, are out of bounds. This book has but a few central messages, but this is one of them: we simply can no longer afford to be led by people wearing ideological blinders. We must seriously investigate a new way of thinking if we are to successfully craft an equitable approach to growth, risk, and the distribution of opportunity and income.

For decades in the post-WWII era, the income of the typical family rose in lockstep with the economy's performance. As the bakers of the economic pie—the workforce—grew more productive, they benefited commensurately from their work: between the mid-1940s and the mid-1970s, both productivity and real median family income doubled.

Since the mid-1970s, however, family income has grown at one-third the rate of productivity, even though families are working harder and longer than ever. Recently, the problem has grown more severe. In late 2003, we finally pulled out of the longest "jobless recovery" on record, going back to the 1930s. Our economy expanded, but we were losing jobs. Moreover, despite solid overall growth since the recession of 2001, the typical family's income has consistently fallen and poverty has gone up. The gap between the growth in productivity, which has been quite stellar, and the very flat pace at which the living standards of most families are improving has never been wider. This is a characteristic of YOYO economics: the economy does fine; the people in the economy do not.

How has this occurred, and what role do the people and politics of YOYO play? While the whole story might be made more interesting by a right-wing conspiracy, the rise of YOYO isn't one. Though conservatives have introduced recent YOYO initiatives like Social Security privatization and private accounts for health care and unemployment, this is not a story of good Democrats and bad Republicans. It is the story of the ascendancy of a largely bipartisan vision that promotes individualist market-based solutions over solutions that recognize there are big problems that markets cannot effectively solve.

We cannot, for example, constantly cut the federal government's revenue stream without undermining its ability to meet pressing social needs. We know that more resources will be needed to meet the challenges of prospering in a global economy, keeping up with technological changes, funding health care and pension systems, helping individuals balance work and family life, improving the skills of our workforce, and reducing social and economic inequality. Yet discussion of this reality is off the table.

WE'RE IN THIS TOGETHER

We need an alternative vision, one that applauds individual freedom but emphasizes that such freedom is best realized with a more collaborative approach to meeting the challenges we face. The message is simple: *We're in this together*. Here, the acronym is *WITT*.

Though this alternative agenda uses the scope and breadth of the federal government to achieve its ends, this book is not a call for more government in the sense of devoting a larger share of our economy to government spending. In fact, there is surprisingly little relationship between the ideological agenda of those in charge and the share of the economy devoted to the federal government. To the contrary, some of the biggest spenders of federal funds have been purveyors of hyper-individualism (with G. W. Bush at the top of the list). But, regardless of what you feel the government's role should be in the economy and society, an objective look at the magnitude of the challenges we face shows we must restore the balance between individual and collective action. We simply cannot effectively address globalization, health care, pensions, economic insecurity, and fiscal train wrecks by cutting taxes, turning things over to the market, and telling our citizens they're on their own, like the gold prospectors of the 1800s, to strike it rich or bust.

All Together Now aims to set us on a new path. At the heart of the WITT agenda is the belief that we can wield the tools of government to build a more just society, one that preserves individualist values while ensuring that the prosperity we generate is equitably shared. Importantly, under the WITT agenda, this outcome occurs not through redistributionist Robin Hood schemes, but through creating an economic architecture that reconnects our strong, flexible economy to the living standards of all, not just to the residents of the penthouse. As the pie grows, all the bakers get bigger slices.

Where YOYO economics explains why we cannot shape our participation in the global economy to meet our own needs, or provide health coverage for the millions who lack that basic right, or raise the living standards of working families when the economy is growing, WITT policies target these challenges head on.

As YOYOism rolls on, the amplitude of our national discomfort, the vague sense that something is fundamentally wrong in how we conduct our national and international affairs, is climbing. In poll after poll, solid majorities view our country as headed in the wrong direction, and there are signs that the YOYO infrastructure is not impenetrable. Though the administration may ultimately get its way, some members of Congress have unexpectedly been resisting White House demands for billions more in tax cuts for the wealthy. In a totally uncharacteristic reversal, the Bush administration was forced to reinstate the prevailing wage rule it suspended in the wake of Hurricane Katrina. In the off-year 2005 elections, a few closely watched races revealed that simply pledging to cut taxes wasn't enough. In a couple of important cases, candidates and initiatives that delivered more WITTisms than YOYOisms prevailed.[1] The climate of a few years ago has changed, and resistance is no longer futile.

A growing chorus is calling for a more balanced role of government in our lives. In the words of Iowa governor Tom Vilsack, "Government is nothing more nor less than the instrument whereby our people come together to undertake collectively the responsibilities we cannot discharge alone." If enough of us add our voices, we can reject messages like "It's your money" and "You're on your own" as divisive and counterproductive.

We can move the pendulum away from a politics that excessively focuses on individuals—the YOYO agenda—toward an approach wherein we work together to craft solutions to the challenges we face. Embedded in these solutions is a healthy respect for markets and individuals. But that respect is not excessive. It does not lead us to stand idly by while the economy expands year after year as poverty rises and the real incomes of working families stagnate. Neither does it impel us to shy away from our goal: building a society where the fruits of economic growth are broadly shared with those who create that growth each day of their working lives.

A RETURN TO COMMON SENSE

The subtitle of this book invokes *Common Sense*, the most famous work of the American revolutionary Thomas Paine. What's the connection?

It's partly, of course, the issue of whom our government represents. Paine was ready to throw off the yoke of British tyranny well before most of the nation's founders were. In this spirit, part of what follows is a common-sense critique of the United States' current situation. As discussed in chapter 1, hyper-individualism has held sway numerous times in our history, and a characteristic of these periods is the extent to which they favor the chosen few over the majority.

But what makes Paine so relevant today was his ability to see outside the box. While the majority of the colonists were unhappy with the Crown, most were unable to envision ending their relationship with England and seriously consider independence. *Common Sense*, which starts right off with a vitriolic personal attack on King George III, offered the colonists a radically different view of their options. Paine told the colonists that their humanity was a gift from God, not from the king. Thus, they had a responsibility to themselves and their children to construct a system of government that would free them from the constraints of the Crown to pursue their "natural rights." We can see this philosophy clearly embedded in the Declaration of Independence, where the right to life, liberty, and the pursuit of happiness was enshrined as a God-given, self-evident right of humanity.

We have drifted too far from Paine's vision. Many of us share a sense of deep discomfort and insecurity about the direction our country is taking. But there do not seem to be any signposts pointing to a better way. Why not?

It's easy to blame the lack of leadership, and there's something to that. The quality of many of our leaders does seem particularly suspect these days. Opportunists can always be found in politics, but their influence is often countered by those truly motivated to promote the public good (which is not to say that such people agree on how to do so, of course). Right now, the ratio of opportunists to idealists may be unusually high.

But the problem cuts deeper. The emphasis on individualism will always be a core American value, but it has been stressed to the breaking point. As the YOYO influence has spread, assisted by the muscular application of contemporary economics (as discussed in chapter 2), the YOYOs have implemented a philosophy of hyper-individualism that disdains using the tools of government to seek solutions. More than anything else, this policy has led to our current predicament. Under the banner of "You're on your own," we have lost a sense of common ownership of our government, an institution that many of us now distrust as feckless at best and corrupt at worst.

This abandonment of our faith in government to help meet the challenges we face—social, economic, and international—has been costly. We have shut off our critical faculties that under normal circumstances would lead us to be deeply angered by much of what's going on. Despite the events of September 11, 2001, we are less prepared for a national disaster now than we were a few years ago. Our citizens are dying in an underfunded war launched on false pretenses, and our actions have helped to unleash powerful forces that are both lethal and destabilizing. A majority of our representatives are addicted to tax cuts with no regard for their future impact. Short-sighted vested interests are at the table, constructing self-enriching energy policies instead of incentives to conserve; polluters are editing the science out of environmental protection acts.

These are front-page stories. Yet in the absence of a broadly shared vision in which we see that each one of these calamities poses a deep threat to our common fate, it's not clear how we should react. We have a vague sense that something important is off-kilter, but since the YOYOs have taken government solutions off the table, we have no means of crafting a suitable response. When the answer for every problem is a market-based solution—a private account, leavened with a tax cut for the wealthiest—we are trapped.

Clearly, we need to escape from that restrictive, cynical vision. Pursuing our collective, rather than strictly personal, interests will help. The plan I offer is straightforward: diagnose the point at which we got off course and chart the way forward.

The diagnosis begins in chapter 1, with a more detailed explanation of YOYO ideas and policies and a brief history of their evolution. Chapter 2 looks at the supporting role played by economists whose ideas in recent years have lent sustenance and support to the YOYO agenda. In chapter 3, I get proactive and lay out the WITT agenda. Chapter 4 addresses a set of challenges to the agenda, and the final chapter concludes with thoughts about how a movement to implement these ideas might be nurtured into being.

My hope is that the ideas that follow, along with some of the great work of others I cite along the way, will morph into a blueprint for such a movement to carry out. By working, thinking, and planning "all together now," we can find our way toward a more hopeful future for ourselves, our families, and our society.

CHAPTER ONE

Risk Shifting, from Coolidge to Katrina

ON AUGUST 29, 2005, the powerful hurricane Katrina hit the U.S. Gulf Coast, flooding 80 percent of New Orleans. An estimated one million people were evacuated from the area, though many of the poor, old, and ill were unable to leave and seek higher ground. Moreover, those left behind were overwhelmingly African American. The nation watched in horror as death and destruction flashed across our TV screens. We were inured to seeing such events unfold in third-world countries. How could they possibly occur in a major American city?

Equally unbelievable, the government response at all levels was late, insufficient, and widely considered by all sides to have been lethally bungled. President Bush, on vacation at the time, appeared not to grasp the magnitude of what was occurring until a day or two later. Even then, he was uncharacteristically off-key in his response. His initial comments that "America will be a stronger place" for going through the disaster seemed like spin, especially given the inadequate federal response.

As the tragedy wore on, the feds and local politicians started blaming each other. The Federal Emergency Management Agency, though created to react to such emergencies, was particularly inept.

As reported by *Los Angeles Times* journalist Peter Gosselin, FEMA underwent a renaissance under Clinton, "speedily responding to the 1993 Mississippi flood, the 1994 Northridge earthquake, and other disasters." When George W. Bush was elected, he gave the job of heading FEMA to his campaign manager, Joe Allbaugh, who criticized his new charge as "an oversized entitlement program," suggesting that states and cities would be better off relying on "faith-based organizations."[1]

Much of the public became transfixed by the disaster and its aftermath. For the media, it was all Katrina, all the time. As an economist who often comments on government data releases, I was asked in every interview about the economic impact of Katrina for weeks after the storm. As the days wore on, we learned to our disbelief about victims dying in homes, in hospitals, and on the flooded streets of their cities, especially New Orleans. It seemed incomprehensible that we as a nation would be unprepared for such an emergency, especially after the terrorist attacks of 9/11.

Right underneath the surface of all this anxiety could be felt the pulse of a critically important national discussion about the role of government. A critique of the political and social philosophy I'm calling YOYO ("You're on your own") coalesced amid the storm's wreckage. To be sure, there were those who dismissed the significance of FEMA's performance as just another example of governmental failure, but these were largely anti-government ideologues whose views appeared to be out of step with the mainstream. Few took seriously the notion that less government was necessary, before or after the event. To the contrary, the conservative majority in the federal government immediately began spending billions (over $60 billion in the first week, with billions more to follow, the most ever in response to a natural disaster) to redress the damage.

A conversation broke out on the op-ed pages, in blogs, in letters to the editor, wherein citizens actively wondered if we'd gone too far down the YOYO path. Liberal columnists like Paul Krugman lambasted the administration, connecting the dots between its ideology of individualism and its failure to rise to an occasion of such dire need. In an op-ed entitled "Killed by Contempt," he wrote:

> The federal government's lethal ineptitude wasn't just a consequence of Mr. Bush's personal inadequacy; it was a consequence of ideological hostility to the very idea of using government to serve the public good. For 25 years the right has been denigrating the public sector, telling us that government is always the problem, not the solution. Why should we be surprised that when we needed a government solution, it wasn't forthcoming? [2]

Letters to the editor during this period express with crystal clarity the stakes invoked by hyper-individualism. One letter argued that this breakdown of the social contract was directly related to the "starve the beast" mentality of those who would cripple the government by cutting off its revenue stream. The writer went on to assert that, contrary to the belief of those in charge, "'the beast' is not government. It is the insolence of those who believe that helping one's fellow citizens is not a duty, but an option." [3]

Another letter writer summed it up this way:

> We have a president . . . and a Congress whose agenda is to privatize risk by reducing public financing and dismantling public safeguards, including bankruptcy, Social Security, health insurance, and environmental and disaster protections.
>
> The level of the government's response to Katrina was as predictable as the hurricane itself. You get what you pay for.
>
> This is what an ownership society looks like. This is what an ownership society means: we are each of us on our own. [4]

Even conservative columnists such as David Brooks talked about the hurricane's aftermath as a unique opportunity to use the tools of government to address the deep economic and social inequities that remained so stark even as the floodwaters receded. [5]

I'm not citing those letters and opinion pieces because I think they're right. I do, but what of it? There are surely letters and op-eds saying just the opposite. I'm citing them because they so precisely capture my point. Even before Katrina, many of us shared a sense that something was wrong with the extent to which we were shifting economic and social risks from shared sources to individuals. The privatization efforts by the government, the defunding of safety nets, the decision of businesses to drop worker pensions, changes in corporate norms that in earlier times protected jobs but now made workers more disposable—all of these ongoing risk shifts were already leading to a heightened sense of YOYO-induced insecurity. But the storm, and particularly its aftermath, shoved these concerns to the front burner for a growing number of citizens.

AFTER THE STORM:
A POTENTIALLY TRANSFORMATIVE MOMENT

Eventually stories of the flood receded from the front page, but the sentiments remained. As I mentioned, part of my job is to debate national economic policy, and I'm well aware that two economists hammering it out on CNBC as to whether the Bush tax cuts really created jobs, or whether the Federal Reserve should raise interest rates, seems more like weird entertainment than something that might yield useful insights. Yet, in the post-Katrina world, the discussion felt a lot more urgent. Suddenly, something important seemed to be riding on whether we could blithely add more than $100 billion to the deficit for rebuilding hurricane-damaged areas while engaging in further tax cuts for the wealthy. All of a sudden, we stumbled upon a potentially transformative moment in history and politics.

After the storm, at least for a while, there was a sense that it matters how we as a nation handle the responsibility of economic policy (and by we I mean the electorate, a bunch of people who collectively decide whom we appoint to set the nation's agenda). It matters how we approach the big problems of the day: globalization, national health care, taxes, our stagnating and ever more unequal incomes. But it also matters how we approach the problems in our everyday lives.

The incredibly uneven quality of our public schools, the eroding quality and cost shifting of employer-provided health care and pensions, the increasing insecurity of all jobs, not just those in manufacturing—all these problems link back to an ongoing shift in the way we view the role of government in our lives. That view has evolved from a mind-set that dates back to the Depression. Under that mind-set, which persisted until about a generation ago, more of us had a greater sense that we're all in this together and that it is our right and our privilege as a society to take the needed steps to ensure our economic security.

We've lost that sense. With the ascendancy of YOYO philosophy, we've lost the ability to come together and create the government we need to meet the economic and social challenges we face at every level. Under YOYO, we can neither shape the way globalization plays out in our lives, nor invest in quality education in our neighborhoods.

It is of course not the only important shift that's occurred. Obviously, our electorate is closely divided along various lines, and I discuss this aspect of the problem in chapter 4 (how can we come together when our views and values seem so different?). But tragedy has a way of pushing our differences into the background. Red stater or blue stater, any one of us could have been caught in that storm, just as any of us could be caught in the sights of terrorists. In Katrina's aftermath, there existed, at least for a few weeks, an uneasy sense that the path down which YOYO politics has been taking us is as dangerous as it is unsustainable. And of course, many of us felt this long before the New Orleans levees gave way.

In this regard, when he asserted that America may well be a stronger place once we recover from this devastating blow, the president may have been right. But ironically, it will be because we once again see the danger in the type of government that his administration, with the help of the Congress, has so aggressively been pursuing. The Katrina debacle was a terrible wake-up call, reminding us of the costs of losing sight of our connections to each other.

THE ATTEMPT TO PRIVATIZE SOCIAL SECURITY: A YOYO CASE STUDY

So that is where we are.

Our response to Katrina exposed the underbelly of the opportunity society and in that sense makes the task of this chapter—to present the drawbacks of such a society—easier. But before we go back in time to explore the roots of hyper-individualism, let's develop a better understanding of the problem by examining a present-day example of YOYO in action: the attempt by the Bush administration to change Social Security from a program that guarantees a benefit to a program that draws at least part of the benefit from a privately held account invested in the stock market.

The plan to partially privatize Social Security by giving individuals the opportunity to invest a portion of their Social Security payroll taxes in financial markets is, or really was, the major economic initiative of President Bush's second term. Under this plan, the government would no longer guarantee a pension; instead, a pension would partially be a function of how well an individual did in the stock market during his or her working years.

In this chapter, the goal is less to critique this idea, and others like it, than to deconstruct it. What characterizes these initiatives and what do they tell us about where their advocates are coming from? Where are these ideas taking us?

As its second term got under way, the administration of President Bush was working tirelessly on selling Social Security reform.

Like a pop star promoting a new CD, the president toured sixty cities to make his case. But other than the handpicked fans that came to the "concerts," the dominant consensus seemed to be that the new tunes weren't very catchy.

Which raises the question: why, after a seemingly endless campaign yielded another narrow victory, did the newly reelected administration turn to a major restructuring of a program so popular with the electorate that it has been called a third rail, "killing" any politician reckless enough to touch it?

The Stated Objections

The "reformers" claimed to be motivated by concerns that Social Security would be unable to meet its financial obligations. But there were two pretty big problems with making this case. First, the program is not in nearly as bad a shape fiscally as its opponents have claimed. It's sound for about forty more years and may require relatively small tweaks thereafter. And second, private accounts don't change the fiscal outlook one bit. It's simple arithmetic: we can address a fiscal shortfall by raising taxes or cutting benefits, and both were off the table.

In fact, the administration never had the chutzpah to put forth a plan. Some administration officials did say they liked a few ideas, including most recently, one that reduces benefits for recipients with higher family incomes. Needless to say, that didn't get very far. One of the treasured aspects of Social Security is its universal application: it's not a "means tested" poverty program. This is an important distinction, because programs for the poor end up being underfunded and politically unpopular. Thus, introducing an income test to Social Security was widely regarded as a back-door attempt to weaken it.

The case against Social Security was also overshadowed by a real wolf at the door: the American health care system. The nonpartisan Congressional Budget Office has made this clear time and again, showing that the combination of an aging society and fast-rising health care costs means that health care spending is slated to sop up much, much more of our future resources than Social Security. (For the record, health care costs are by no means a burden only for the public sector; they are an equally serious problem in the private sector.) And let's face it, whatever you believe about Social Security's finances, the tax-and-spend policies of the Bush administration do not reveal much concern for fiscal sanity. Why, then, should its officials come out swinging so hard against Social Security?

The fact is that Social Security has long been in the YOYOs' sights. While federal health care spending will grow much faster than Social Security in the coming years, Social Security has characteristics that keep hyper-individualists up at night.

The Real Objections

First, it's a big government program on which many people depend. We spent about half a trillion bucks on Social Security in 2004, accounting for more than 20 percent of government expenditures that year. Social Security is the main source of income for two-thirds of the elderly. For YOYOs seeking to eviscerate the government, such a huge program, no matter how popular, is too important a target to ignore.

But it's the very idea of Social Security that really goads them. Social Security takes a universal challenge—the need to protect the vulnerable (the program officially insures against old age, disability, and the loss of a spouse, but for brevity, I'll just refer to the old-age component)—and shares the responsibility of meeting it among members of the working generation, whose income supports the aged.

Though I grant you that we rarely discuss it in these terms, Social

Security creates a strong link between the aged and the working-age population. The idea behind the program is that today's workers create the capital, the technology, and the wealth that will support tomorrow's generation. Embedded in its mind-numbing formulas is the notion that those of us who came before, whether they were teachers, accountants, homemakers, mail carriers, barbers, cashiers, or lawyers, have built up the productive capacity of our nation. When the children of these workers come of age (along with new immigrants), they will earn their living from this infrastructure while also making their own contributions. As they do so, we will peel off some portion of their earnings to provide pensions for their forebears, just as those forebears did for their own predecessors. If this were a Disney movie, music about the "Circle of Life" would swell up here, but suffice it to say, Social Security is an elegant collaborative solution to a universal challenge.

The YOYOs want to put a stop to all this cozy intergenerational sharing. Instead of using today's earnings to pay for today's retirees, they want you to be able to invest a portion of your Social Security payroll taxes into a go-it-alone "individual account."[6] Thus, Social Security stands as a testament to the benefits of collective action, of pooling the risks associated with becoming too old to work, or losing a spouse, or becoming disabled. Private accounts, conversely, are a great example of the "You're on your own" approach to these causes of income loss. Some people would come out ahead under such a scheme, but many would not, and those with the lowest incomes and the least investment acumen (or the least time and the fewest resources to develop such acumen) would be least likely to benefit.

Moreover, according to the work of economist Robert Shiller, it's likely that the majority of retirees would end up with a less economically secure pension than they have under the current system.[7] It's not that the stock market is always a worse bet than the reliable, albeit boring, Social Security investment in government bonds, the safest vehicle on the road. It's really more a tortoise-and-hare situation.

For most people, the slow and steady investment in government bonds under the current system yields higher returns at retirement than the stock market would. One reason is that the need for a pension grows with the age of the worker. Thus, if the employee/investor is unlucky enough to hit retirement age during a down market, too bad. Sure, it might be possible to keep working and investing, but down markets can last years. The bottom line: most people don't want to gamble with their pensions, which is why the private-account campaign has been such a bust for the YOYOs.

One researcher, for example, examined the hypothetical case of someone who retired at age sixty-five in 2000 (when financial markets were booming) versus another who retired in 2003 (when they were tanking). After forty years of investing 6 percent of his salary in a 401(k)-type plan and retiring in 2000, Happy Joe Boom could have bought an annuity that would give him 134 percent of his pre-retirement income per month for the rest of his life. But Sad John Bust, who made the same investments but retired three years later, would receive only 57 percent.[8]

In this same spirit of risk aversion, it's also worth noting that Social Security as currently structured provides benefits until death. You can outlive the returns from a private account.

Now, I wasn't there when the administration officials came up with the idea of selling privatized Social Security. But I'll bet the possibility that private accounts could underperform the current universal "We're in this together" system, with its publicly held assets, never occurred to them. The YOYO ideology led these officials to assume that you're always better off when you're out for yourself. The idea of dismantling the "third rail"—to create millions of independent investors while surgically removing the collectivist heart of a policy that connects Americans across generations—also had appeal. YOYOs are unsettled by a system wherein the retirement of today's older generation is financed by a new immigrant working a construction site as well as a young urban professional beginning a career in finance.

It's revealing that this latter point has not been the line of defense for keeping the program intact. Instead, those against privatization have promoted the work of analysts, like Shiller, who show that relative to the current system, individual investors could lose a hefty chunk of their retirement funds in the market.

I'm not sure why no one thought to tap Social Security's collective risk-sharing aspects in its defense. Maybe they tried it and it polled badly with a focus group. But I doubt it. It may be the case that those who oppose privatization (and who argue at most for small alterations to the current program) are stuck in the dominant frame of "What's better for me?" That is, they probably believed that they'd never convince the general population with arguments about pooling everyone's risk under the banner of intergenerational interdependence. So they never proposed the alternative frame: We're all in this together; we've all got productive years and retirement years ahead of us; there's a time to sow and a time to reap. How, then, can we best come together to tap our resources to meet this challenge?

I readily grant that the other frame—"What's better for me?"—is by no means unappealing, and the interesting question for someone of my persuasion is, what if the numbers had worked out differently? What if they had showed that a privatized system did yield better results? In that case I'd move to a hybrid that tapped the power of the market but preserved the core collective aspect of Social Security.[9] Once the program is privatized, once one huge pool becomes a million puddles, something inherent that binds us together is lost. A privatized program would chip away at our fundamental connectedness. Under such a system, when I walk down the street as an aging baby boomer, I would no longer see younger generations contributing to my old age while building the economy for the progeny of their fellow citizens. I would see a bunch of competitors in the stock market.

OTHER YOYO INITIATIVES: KNOW THEM WHEN YOU SEE THEM

Social Security reform is the most visible example of where the hyper-individualists want to take us, but the promotion of Health Savings Accounts is an equally telling example of their thinking. As described in fascinating detail in an article by Malcolm Gladwell in *The New Yorker*, the idea of HSAs is to shift the risk of paying for illness from the largest pool to the smallest, from society at large to individuals.[10]

HSAs are already on the books, although, like the idea of injecting private accounts into Social Security, they're not very popular. They work by setting up an individual account—see the pattern?— where you can deposit money, tax free, to use for health care. If you're young and healthy, or think you are, you can use the money to pay for that rare visit to the doctor while your account grows, since you can invest the account funds just like IRAs. The plan also requires that you own a low-premium, high-deductible insurance plan against "catastrophic illness."

The way the YOYOs see it, the plan will save the system money by shifting more costs from the insurer to the "health care consumer," or sick person, thus providing a new disincentive to go the doctor (as though you need another one). Essentially, the plan gives individuals an incentive to gamble: if they stay well, they can save tax free. But if they fall ill before they've had time to accumulate much in the account, they're going to be worse off than if they'd stuck with a typical plan under the current system. Interestingly, the early research shows that this is precisely what's happening: people in HSAs spend more on out-of-pocket expenses and premiums than people in traditional plans.[11]

Let's look for a moment at what the Social Security and HSA plans share. In fact, a few core themes emerge that are useful markers for recognizing YOYO initiatives. Both deal with significant risks: in the case of Social Security, old age (and disability and the loss of a spouse); in the case of HSAs, illness. Both plans meet these risks by encouraging individuals to manage their own accounts, building up the reserves they need to finance their own retirement or health care needs.

The first thing to notice is that both plans rely heavily on the market. They work off the assumption that if individuals are given the right incentives, two things will happen: people will take the necessary steps to meet the risks in question, and the market will respond appropriately. In the case of Social Security, that response equals an investment portfolio that reliably beats the current system (which it doesn't, as Shiller has shown).

With the health accounts, the idea is to make consumers better shoppers. In a speech touting this aspect of the policy, President Bush argued that there's not enough "comparative shopping" in health care, noting that you wouldn't shop for tile or insulation that way. "You don't know whether the guy next is going to offer a better deal when it comes to some kind of medical procedure," he said.[12] Later we'll discuss the huge inefficiencies triggered by this approach, but here, the point is to see the YOYOs' fundamental belief that health care is just another commodity to be priced on the open market. They believe that what's driving health costs is too much insurance held by too many people who are not conscious enough about cost savings. The idea behind HSAs is that the actions of account holders will create the competition needed to drive down prices and provide a better set of choices for consumers.

Never mind that trying to meld health care and markets got us deep into this mess in the first place, that health care ain't tile, that every other advanced economy has solved this conundrum with universal coverage, that it doesn't make sense to give people an incentive to put off going to the doctor, or that those with low incomes will be hard-pressed to build the account or meet the high deductible. And never mind that HSAs can't really control costs anyway, because the big spending in health care is for the expensive procedures that will always be covered by insurance. No one's going to pay for heart surgery out of pocket. For YOYOs, it's all markets, all the time, and don't let the facts get in the way.

Second, such initiatives aim to shrink the role of government. YOYOs don't just rely on the market; they generally also view government with outright hostility. Some of this is only in theory: they spend a lot of federal dollars despite their rhetoric. But their rap clearly casts government as an impediment to be gotten around. Granted, that opinion is not exceptional these days, as most Americans are quite skeptical of the government's ability to act efficiently, a skepticism boosted almost monthly (think Katrina).

And that's exactly the way the YOYOs want it. It's another important theme we'll see popping up throughout: if you're running the shop, it's not that hard to prove to your constituency that government is ineffective. You staff it with incompetents, slash its income, decry it from the bully pulpit, and sit back and watch your self-fulfilling prophecy come true.

A related theme here, one that comes out in the brief history that follows, is that, in contrast to their mistrust of government solutions, YOYOs have a reverence for corporate solutions. They reflexively believe that private firms, acting in their own interest, will promote the wider interests of society as well.

Third, YOYO initiatives avoid sharing resources and risks. To the contrary, they create individual silos. Clearly, a goal of their policies is to put the individual, not the group, at the center of the solution. This grows out of their faith in incentives. The hyper-individualist fears that pooling risks erodes a person's incentive to meet risks. People provided with universal health care, for example, will have less reason to take better care of themselves and avoid frivolous uses of the system. (Jargon alert: economists call this proclivity "moral hazard," which occurs when insurance allegedly leads you to engage in riskier or more expensive behavior than you otherwise would.)

Another YOYO account-based initiative, Personal Reemployment Accounts, floated by the Bush administration in 2003, also reflects this theme. Although Congress opposed the creation of PRAs at the time, they recently resurfaced as part of the administration's plan to rebuild the Gulf Coast.

These accounts were designed with the belief, one supported by some evidence, that people receiving unemployment insurance aren't always in a rush to find a new job.[13] The PRA thus establishes an account for the job seeker that can be spent on employment-related activities, like job training or career counseling. An unemployed worker who finds a job before exhausting the account gets to keep the difference. Clearly, this approach is designed to counteract the moral hazard in the current unemployment insurance system.

Finally, there's the personal anti-terrorism account . . . Just kidding, but the pattern is incredibly clear.

These initiatives sound pretty reasonable, no? The classically trained economists have probably all bailed out by now, but if any are still with us, they're probably thinking these ideas make some sense. Yet, as the lack of acceptance of these ideas reveals, the people feel otherwise.

And the people have got it right. The three principles cited above—freer markets, less government, and more individualism— are fundamentally flawed when it comes to retirement, health care, and unemployment, not to mention the slew of other big-ticket challenges we face, like globalization and rising inequality.

The YOYOs get it wrong because they mistakenly ascribe the source of both the problem and the solution to the individual. But these challenges are bigger than an individual's ability to fix them, even for him- or herself. Take unemployment: while the traditional unemployment insurance program implicitly assumes the problem is on the demand side—there are too few jobs—the PRA embeds the notion that what stands between an individual and a new job is her reluctance to get off the dole and get to work. In the real world, where a weekly benefit check replaces about half an average worker's earnings, most families can't rely on unemployment insurance to make up for lost wages. What has held such job seekers back, especially in the absence of tight labor markets over the past thirty years (a tight labor market is one with very low unemployment), isn't the enticement of a benefit check nearly as much as it is the scarcity of decent jobs. By obsessively focusing on the moral hazard, the YOYOs aim their policy fix at the individual and miss the real target: the lack of good job opportunities.

There is of course a place for tapping the immense and creative powers of the private market, for sending out accurate "price signals," for worrying about moral hazards, and for getting the individual incentives right. But that place is not around health care, pensions, unemployment, and a slew of other risk-laden issues that loom large in today's economy.

What is it about these particular aspects of our economic lives that makes them inadequate candidates for market solutions? For one, they are areas of the human experience that entail risks we all share, and even if we don't experience them—if we never fall seriously ill or experience a spell of unemployment—our economic security is greatly enhanced if there's a safety net in place. You might hope that the private market would respond to this need, but that turns out to be both impossible (because some people simply can't afford to purchase a personal safety net) and highly inefficient (because the benefits of very large risk pools are lost).

Second, markets fail, and they fail at many levels. There are big-time market failures like stock market or housing bubbles, massive layoffs, and recessions. Then there are the midlevel failures, ones that may not throw the economy off track but will certainly entail huge costs for their victims. I'm thinking here of firms that go bankrupt and renege on their pension promises, or industries hard-pressed to compete in global markets where the deck is stacked against them. (U.S. manufacturers face a huge disadvantage when Asian countries manipulate their currencies to make our exports more expensive, for example.) Then there are the everyday failures, like the lack of health care coverage for about 75 percent of the jobs in the low-wage labor market, or the steady pace of layoffs, now more numerous even in good economic times.

Third, these areas involve social goods, and you can't count on the markets to price or provide them at a level that will work best for most of us. If you want to accurately price future options on pork bellies, the market is your best bet. If you want to set the right price for access to health care, look elsewhere.

As discussed next, history shows that these matters are best dealt with either outside the market, by pooling both risks and responsibilities, or inside the market, but with a dose of regulation to steer it in a direction that works best for the most people. History also shows that when we've tried to ignore this lesson, we generate astounding levels of inequality—of wealth, income, and opportunity.

HOW EVER DID WE GET HERE?

One could view the history of economic and social policy in America through the lens of the tension between YOYO ("You're on your own") and WITT ("We're in this together"). In each period we seem to locate ourselves somewhere on the continuum between them, and whenever we go too far to one side, we slide back to the other.

Contemporary social policy begins in the 1920s, a period that has much in common with what we're living through today. A few decades before then, as the Industrial Revolution hit its stride, America was introduced to the new captains of industry, people like Andrew Carnegie and John D. Rockefeller. The political power of these unimaginably successful industrialists—their ability to determine the standard of living for millions of Americans—caught the attention of muckraking journalists, progressive policy types like Louis Brandeis, and President Theodore Roosevelt, whose administration brought a large number of antitrust suits against these men (the most memorable being the 1911 case that broke Rockefeller's Standard Oil monopoly).

Yet once this burst of progressive regulation played out, the tide began to turn toward the unregulated accumulation of wealth. The sensibility of the time was that the muckrakers and regulators thoughtlessly (or in the minds of some, socialistically) handcuffed the "invisible hand" of free-market economics. Regulatory commissions were denounced by Republican leaders, and President Coolidge summed it up with his famous declaration that "the chief business of the American people is business."

What ensued was the largest increase in the concentration of wealth in the history of the data, and almost surely in the history of our country. As figure 1.1 shows, the 1920s era of wealth accumulation has only one competitor: our own era.[14]

There's a lot to be said about this trend. Why does it occur? What is responsible for the peaks and valleys of inequality? Why is inequality a problem? I will address those questions later, but for now it is important to recognize some characteristics that the two periods share.

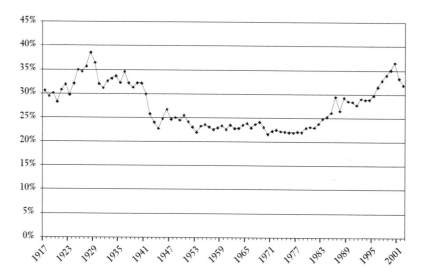

FIGURE 1.1
The share of the nation's income going to
the top 5 percent of the population, 1917–2002.

[SOURCE: Thomas Piketty and Emmanuel Saez, "Income Inequality in the United
States, 1913–1998," *Quarterly Journal of Economics* 118, no. 1 (February 2003): 1–39.]

Most significantly, in both the 1920s and the 1980s, when the gap
between rich and poor began to widen, the federal government
consciously constrained its regulatory role, allegedly to promote
business interests. Regulations to prevent monopoly power in the
earlier period, or to set minimum wages, preserve union power, or
provide welfare or unemployment insurance benefits in the latter
era, were denounced as doing more harm than good. If only the
chains of socialist regulation could be broken, it was said, the
unleashed power of the market economy would provide for all.

What about this claim? Figure 1.1 shows these sentiments to be
closely tied to sharp spikes in inequality, but that could be an ancil-
lary effect of the economic turbocharge that the deregulators take
credit for. Yet the evidence doesn't support their claims at all. It

never has. It takes about an hour on the Internet to collect the relevant statistics. The United States' bottom line, the gross domestic product, did not grow faster during those periods, nor did employment, investment, or most importantly, productivity, the measure most associated with a successful economy.

To spare you a statistical pit stop, I've relegated to the appendix the evidence comparing the growth rates of these variables over different periods. There you will see that during periods wherein large, regressive tax cuts were sold as ways to promote faster investment, better job growth, and higher productivity, the cuts didn't have those effects at all. In the Reagan and Bush II eras, YOYO economics generated annual GDP growth rates of 3 percent and 2.6 percent, the lowest in the table, with data going back to 1949. Same for investment growth, same for employment growth. Worst of all, those years saw the slowest growth of real income for the typical (that is, the median-income) family.

I won't go so far as to claim this is a slam dunk against the cheerleaders for the freest possible market. They can, and do, make all kinds of arguments about why such simple comparisons are inadequate. Any economy always has millions of moving parts, and one could argue that productivity growth over the Reagan years never took off because . . . well, I can't think of why, but I'm sure someone has.

But here is the slam-dunk, hole-in-one, surefire case made by these historical comparisons: YOYO policies—massive tax cuts for rich people, privatization, deregulation—are unequivocally not associated with better macroeconomic outcomes. They demonstrably have not led to faster growth, in terms of GDP, employment, or productivity. What they have done, at least in the two periods highlighted above, is led to huge redistributions of wealth.

And wealth isn't the only thing redistributed during these periods. Economic risk was also shifted squarely onto the shoulders of the less advantaged. As the rules and norms of those eras evolved, the less economic or political clout a person had, the less he or she was insulated from the inevitable upheavals of a deregulated economy.

The greatest cataclysm of all, the Great Depression, followed the excesses of the 1920s, and it gave rise to a very different approach to managing economic risk. Few need reminding of the conditions of that era, when unemployment, hunger, and homelessness soared to unprecedented heights. The majority of Americans came to understand that we needed to pool some amount of our resources to do a better job of looking out for one another.

But memories of this era have faded, and while there still exists considerable poverty amid the plenty in America, we've seen nothing like the devastating economic conditions of the 1930s. As our collective memories fade, opportunistic YOYOs have built a movement to reverse the policies that reflect the shared values that grew out of that era. The results can be seen in the inequality trends above, and in the unwillingness and inability of government to face the pressing challenges of the day. But even though this profound policy shift is very much upon us, its nature is not always obvious. We are thus lucky that some clever and dedicated people have recognized the problem and are documenting it.

RISK SHIFT: THE YOYOS' MODUS OPERANDI

Much like Gottfried Leibniz and Isaac Newton, who, working separately, discovered the calculus at the same time, an economics reporter and a Yale professor discovered that a historically important shift was occurring regarding economic risk. Over the last few decades, a period when the accelerated pace of globalization and technological change was ratcheting up economic insecurity, the government programs, corporate practices, and cultural norms that provided insulation from such insecurities sharply diminished. The result was a huge shift in risk from these larger bodies to individuals.

In 2004, Peter Gosselin of the *Los Angeles Times* began an eye-opening exposé of this phenomenon, entitled "The New Deal." (For this series Gosselin won the Hillman Prize, an award for exploring social justice issues relevant to the common good.) The articles question why so many Americans' sense of economic insecurity has expanded during an era when our nation has grown more prosperous. "The answer," Gosselin wrote, "lies in a quarter-century-long shift of economic risks from the broad shoulders of business and government to the backs of working families. Safety nets that once protected Americans from economic turbulence—safeguards like unemployment compensation and employer loyalty—have eroded or vanished."

As he tracks the evolution of the YOYO vision over the past few decades, Gosselin documents how its policies have exposed more and more individuals and their families to the risks inherent in our economy, including less secure employment, less reliable income trajectories (that is, more ups and downs than in previous periods), worse pension and health coverage, and less reliable public services. The result: the families he follows "are more vulnerable to sudden shifts in the economy than any time since the Great Depression. The result is a daunting 'New Deal' for many working Americans—one that compels them to cope, largely on their own, with financial forces far beyond their control." [15]

In *The Great Risk Shift*, political scientist Jacob Hacker begins with a discovery that family income has become much more volatile in recent decades, jumping up and down much more than it used to. That's a sign that something new and important is buffeting the living standards of working families. When Hacker goes looking for causes, here is what he finds:

> In the past generation, in a wide range of areas—from health care and retirement planning to the job market and the balancing of work and family—the responsibility for economic risk has shifted

from the government and corporations to workers and their families. Some of this shift has been deliberate. Witness the steady cutbacks in workplace health insurance, and corporations' movements away from offering traditional guaranteed pensions in favor of offering "defined-contribution plans" that place the investment risk on workers. Yet a good deal of the Great Risk Shift results not from action, but from *inaction*—from the failure of the government and the corporate sector to accommodate new social and economic realities, leaving families to bear the resulting risks on their own.[16]

Note that Gosselin and Hacker were writing about this phenomenon well before the administration of George W. Bush was offering future Social Security recipients the chance to play the stock market with what would otherwise be a guaranteed pension. And, of course, neither had any idea that a force-five hurricane would collide with years of YOYO politics to expose its inherent contradictions.

As I write the closing words to this chapter, our nation is debating exactly these issues of risk shifting. And as I cited above, the op-eds and letters to the editor are replete with warnings about where the YOYOs are leading us. None of this, however, means we are at a turning point.

The YOYO agenda is creeping back into place. Prior to Hurricane Katrina, Congress was planning to come back from its summer recess and cut $70 billion worth of taxes on dividends and capital gains, make the estate tax cut permanent (a tax that reaches the tiniest sliver of the richest of the rich), while also cutting $40 billion in Medicaid (health insurance for the poor), food stamps, child-support enforcement, student aid, and skill-enhancement programs for workers in need of retraining. The optics of the post-Katrina moment were such that the Congress shelved those ideas for a while. But this type of fiscal policy is pure YOYO—cut taxes for the wealthy and spending on the poor—and it was back for Congress's consideration about six weeks after the storm.

Fear not. Later chapters focus on what needs to happen to push those ideas back off the table. But to put a stake through a bad idea's heart, you need to know where it gets its strength. It turns out that the discipline of economics has evolved in such a way as to form the intellectual underpinnings of YOYO. We turn now to an examination of the way in which these two highly potent forces have come to interact.

CHAPTER TWO

The Economist behind the Curtain

SO A PHYSICIST, an engineer, and an economist find themselves shipwrecked on an island, and their only food is a can of tuna. As they have no tools, they have to figure out how to open it. They each work quietly on the problem for a few minutes and then present their findings to each other.

The physicist begins, "If one of us climbs seventeen feet up that tree and throws the can at that rock with an initial trajectory of 57 degrees . . . ," and so on. The engineer breaks in and alters the trajectory slightly, arguing that the impact must be enough to open the can without splattering its contents. Finally, they turn to the economist and ask for his contribution. His reply: "Assume a can opener . . ."

ASSUME A YOYO ECONOMIST

Economics, often listed in college catalogs under the heading "social science," is a unique science. It does not, like the so-called hard sciences of math or physics, progress toward objective truths about reality. Unlike those sciences, it is based on assumptions about how "economic actors," or people, behave with regard to activities such as saving, consuming, investing, and so on. Its laws, like the "law of one price," are unlike the laws of physics, such as the law of gravity. The latter is a pervasive physical reality. The former is based on a logical assumption—the same good should cost the same everywhere in the same area—but at least where I live, I see it broken every time I drive down the street and pass a few gas stations.

Given its scientific softness, economics tends to have a strong ideological component, and for the last few decades, it has taken a conservative turn. But before then, from the Depression to the Carter years, the discipline of economics looked quite different, as did its implications for the society that applied its insights.

This shift in ideology is not merely of academic interest. Not to put too fine a point on it, economic policy has been instrumental in the demise of WITT and the rise of YOYO. That change was not ordained from above (or below). Neither has it been simply an intellectual evolution, as new ideas and evidence supplant the old. The shift in economic ideology has strong political roots and an even stronger class bias. Filtered through our particular brand of heavily money-laden politics, today's economics supports outcomes much more favorable to the very wealthy and the very politically connected than the tradition it replaced.

The Revenge of the Nerds

Economists, especially those who work for politicians or lobbyists, can be powerful people in an advanced economy like ours. Alan Greenspan, for nearly two decades the chairman of the Federal Reserve, arguably became more powerful than the president on matters economic. By throwing their support one way or the other, economists in high places can affect the lives of millions, both today and in years to come. The decisions they influence—to support or oppose a policy to lower taxes or to build up massive federal budget deficits—can reverberate over generations.

To take but one example, when Greenspan threw his support

behind the massive Bush tax cuts in the early 2000s, their passage became assured. Any lawmakers who were wavering about the wisdom of slashing the government's revenue so dramatically were knocked off the fence once Greenspan weighed in. Now we're stuck with budget deficits that are already hobbling the government's ability to meet pressing social needs. Citing the very deficits they created by enacting those tax cuts, Congress has begun to cut funding for Medicaid, the system of public health care provision for the poorest Americans, even as the rolls of both the poor and the uninsured continue to climb.

These problems will only get worse if we fail to correct the damage and replace the lost revenue. The situation is not entirely Greenspan's fault, in that he didn't propose the tax cuts, but his fingerprints are all over the structural deficits.[1] The result is that Congress can't stop trying to pass more tax cuts—"Hey, Greenspan said we could"—while arguing that the deficits mandate spending cuts in Medicaid, food stamps, worker training, and college aid. It's a potent example of the destructive power of the intersection of these two ideologies: contemporary economics and YOYO.

Different Goals, Different Questions

As explained below, since about the mid-1970s some conservative economists and their university departments helped shift the focus of economics. In broad terms, the old economics had two main policy goals: (1) ensuring that we as a society tap our collective potential and fully employ our economic resources, especially people, and (2) providing individuals with ample protections and publicly provided insurance against undesirable market outcomes—weak job creation, high unemployment, rising poverty rates, and falling real incomes—and other challenges like aging out of the workforce or becoming disabled.

Today's economics also has two goals: (1) getting rid of the policy set associated with the old economics and (2) making sure that individuals are offered the optimal incentives, the ones that should lead them to behave in ways that, according to the mathematical models, bring about the most efficient results.

When the goal of economic policy makers shifted from full employment for the society to the optimal incentives for the individual, YOYO was born. Today, we're seeing the outcomes: greater inequality, a fiscally bankrupt government, the shifting of risk from the government and the firm to the individual, and the loss of the systems and institutions—like pension coverage, minimum wages, overtime rules, and a durable safety net—that insulated workers from market failures and inequities.

With this change in the thrust of economic thinking, the central question of economic policy went from, What can government do to be sure that everyone can contribute to and benefit from the available resources? to, What can government do to get out of the way? The former question considers the challenges inherent in national economies since Adam (Smith, of course) and points to collaborative solutions; the latter, especially when mixed with our unique brand of heavily lobbied government, ignores workers except to tell them, "You're on your own. Here's a tax cut. Now go out there and optimize."

It is extremely unlikely that we as a society will be able to implement WITT policies under the current economic regime. What's needed is a shift in the way we talk, think, and plan for dealing with the risks and opportunities in today's economy. The first step to building an All Together Now movement requires exposing the class biases inherent in YOYO economics and stressing the advantages of a different approach to government, economic policy, and risk sharing. A brief history of how we got to the present state of affairs should help set the stage.

FROM KEYNES TO TODAY: A QUICK AND PAINLESS TOUR

Prior to the Great Depression, economics was far more laissez-faire than it is today. Until his recent retirement, one of the most powerful persons in the world was a crusty central banker named Greenspan. A word from this oracle with thick glasses moved international markets (once you figured out what he was talking about—he's a master of elliptical speech), and presidents had to seek his approval for their economic plans. But the Federal Reserve Bank did not exist at the beginning of the twentieth century: it was created in 1913 to regulate banks more strictly and to give the government more control over economic variables such as interest rates and the money supply. As noted previously, early progressives like Louis Brandeis played a key role in promoting such market regulations, but by the 1920s, the idea that the government should intervene in the markets to ensure a better collective outcome was well out of vogue.

So, when economic tragedy struck, beginning with the market crash in 1929, policy makers did not react, assuming the system would self-correct, or they made mistakes like erecting trade barriers and raising taxes. The Federal Reserve essentially stood by while thousands of banks failed, ensuring that the slump would become the deepest in our history. As a result, we suffered unheard-of levels of unemployment. Today, economic downturns tend to be associated with jobless rates of 7 to 10 percent. Then, measured unemployment surpassed 25 percent, but even that value presents too rosy a picture of the extent of privation.

From an economic perspective, this meant a vast underutilization of human resources. Economic science, however, had yet to evolve to a point where we knew how to correct that imbalance.

Enter the great British economist John Maynard Keynes.

Keynes plays an important role in this story. In helping to construct an economic system to respond to the internationally pervasive slump of the 1930s, his response had something in common with that of Paine to the question of independence. Both men recognized that the institutional systems in place were failing to adequately and fairly serve the collective good, and both recognized that "times that try men's souls," in Paine's words, call for a radical departure from business as usual. While the Keynesian revolution was a far tamer affair than the American one, both men were responsible for major leaps forward in the quest for realizing human potential.

It was then generally believed that left to its own devices, an "invisible hand" would guide the market economy to the best outcomes, including the highest achievable growth rates, enough jobs for those who wanted to work, and incomes that grew with the economy's productivity. Sure, you needed property rights and other legal protections, but once they were in place, rational economic agents would engage with each other in ways that would automatically produce the best results for all parties. Any interventions, including well-intentioned efforts to help the downtrodden, would only lead to counterproductive market distortions, including layoffs, spiraling price increases, and slower real growth. (Keep these ideas in the back of your mind, because they form the basis of today's approach to economics, labeled "neoclassical," because it harks back to these earlier days.)

Keynes, however, looked out at the ravaged landscape of the 1930s and realized that sometimes the invisible hand is all thumbs. His key insight was that left to their own devices, economies like ours as often as not fail to effectively utilize their available resources, including people, an insight that came pretty easy when unemployment had passed 25 percent and poverty was rampant. Keynes and his followers thus rejected a reflexively anti-interventionist stance in favor of a more active approach that would look for ways to push the invisible hand around a bit, specifically through managing the business cycle with fiscal, monetary, and safety-net policies, including the direct creation of jobs by the government itself when labor demand was inadequate.

The Arrival of WITT

To this day, we're arguing about whether Keynes was right. But back in the 1930s, it became a no-brainer that Keynesian economics was the best way forward. Something had to be done. Franklin D. Roosevelt, who had run against Hoover's budget deficits in 1932, initially resisted Keynes's logic, and when the president and Keynes met in 1934, they appear to have mostly perplexed each other. Yet, as the Depression wore on, Roosevelt implemented a Keynesian program. The "alphabet soup" agencies—the NRA, WPA, CCC, and others—were designed to promote public works, rebuild the nation's infrastructure, and reduce unemployment. But those years also saw the creation of lasting set of federal policies that fit perfectly under the banner of "We're in this together," or WITT. Social Security for the elderly, unemployment insurance, a federally mandated minimum wage, collective-bargaining rights for workers, the first federal safety net for the poor—those were the policies of the day.

The aim of those policies was to share risks, to combine our resources to protect the most vulnerable from pervasive and frequent market failures. It was the exact opposite of the intention today. Some of what we are currently debating, like Social Security "reform," is an unabashed attempt to reverse course. As noted in chapter 1, the current Bush team tried to do the same thing with unemployment insurance, turning it into personal accounts to be managed by the unemployed. Although even the Republican-dominated Congress tried to stop them, administration officials successfully went after time-and-a-half pay for overtime work, instituted during the Roosevelt era. In the wake of Hurricane Katrina, they suspended the Davis-Bacon Act of 1931, a rule that prevailing wages must be paid on government-funded projects. (Congress later forced the administration to reverse the suspension.) Those actions took place in broad daylight. Others, like allowing inflation to whittle away at the federal minimum wage until it has become almost meaningless, have been stealth attacks.

YOYOs will argue that Keynesian policies or any similar ideas that intervene in private markets are incompatible with freewheeling global economics. But the policies currently under siege do not pool risk—the risk of unemployment, of an impoverished old age, of large government contractors undermining market wages—for sentimental reasons. They also constitute good economic policy, in the "WITTian" sense that they do not accept undesirable market outcomes, like weak job creation, falling real wages, and insecure retirement, regardless of their cost to society. They help shape market outcomes to achieve two of the central goals of a WITT society: to provide ample and gainful job opportunities and to pool risk across large numbers and thus efficiently protect individuals against market failures. At the same time, they don't assume that the level of economic activity—the extent of consumer demand or the number of available jobs, for example—is ordained from on high and must not be messed with.

On this point, ensuring full employment, Keynes was first and last a hard-nosed macroeconomist: that is, he considered the effects of the policy on society as a whole. Thus, he was motivated by the basic economic principle of fully utilizing the available resources. Far from being incompatible with today's economic landscape, this principle is especially crucial now. Increased trade between nations creates many positive economic opportunities for the citizens of those nations, but in our country, global trade is draining too much demand from our markets, especially our labor market. It is absolutely possible—in fact, it's essential—to craft policies to counteract this effect. As I stress in the next chapter, these ideas are not about reducing global trade. They are designed to replace the demand sapped by such trade, a principle as valid today as it was when Keynes first introduced it.

It would be easy to dismiss WITT economics as the warm and fuzzy preferences of soft-headed liberals but for the fact that these policies accomplish the basic goals of society — economic security and rising living standards — more effectively than YOYO does.

Paradoxically, by clearing the path of the barriers that stand between individuals and their potential, WITT policies facilitate American individualism more than the hyper-individualist YOYO approach, which concentrates resources among those at the top of wealth scale. YOYO policy makers are urged to ignore the plight of individuals stuck in long-term unemployment, an impoverished retirement, or poverty (excepting short periods when natural disasters put them on the front page). WITT policy makers actively pursue measures to reemploy the jobless, provide opportunities to the poor to overcome the barriers they face, and pool resources to enrich the later years of those who have earned the right to a secure retirement.

The Great Depression provides a critical lesson that forms the core of WITT political philosophy. Individuals, families, and communities need economic security to realize their potential, and thus, that should be one of government's core functions. At the heart of contemporary conservatism is the desire to get the government to "leave us alone," so we can live the lives we choose. At the heart of WITT is society's desire to undertake to solve the challenges we face, so that we can live the lives we choose. Of course, YOYO conservatism has convinced the majority that government cannot solve problems but can only make them worse, and this view is obviously inconsistent with the WITT agenda. As discussed next, it is also inconsistent with reality.

The Rise of Incentive-Based Economics

In the 1970s, the collision of painful economic events and the ascendancy of some very conservative economists discredited Keynes's ideas. By stimulating a weak economy, Keynesian management is supposed to reduce unemployment. If it pushes too far, however, it can overheat the economy, leading to faster price increases. So Keynesian economists, perhaps in an overconfident mode, began in the 1960s to talk about calibrating, or fine-tuning, the economy between the two extremes of too little economic heat (producing weak job creation and high unemployment) and too much heat (producing excessive demand that leads to uncomfortable levels of wage and price inflation). Such hubris came under attack by economists like Milton Friedman, who argued that Keynesian interventions interfered in the movements of the invisible hand and would thus do more harm than good.

Enough time had passed since the Depression that it was possible to generate such opposition. Then, right on cue, we entered a trying period of "stagflation" (high inflation and high unemployment), two characters that are not supposed to show up on the same stage. Even though it is now clear that this condition had more to do with a sharp increase in the price of foreign oil than Keynesian efforts to stimulate the economy, a loud chorus of "told you so" resounded from economics departments across the country.

But again, this story is not just one of academic interest. The changing of the intellectual guard did not simply mean that a new generation of grad students was subjected to a different set of equations and theorems. The rise of individual-focused economics was a perfect intellectual complement to the rise of risk-shifting YOYO politicians, whose ascendancy continues to shape our lives in harmful ways.

Jimmy Carter appeared flummoxed by the economic (and global) challenges of the late 1970s, and Ronald Reagan, with his "get the government off our backs" platform, showed up to put the nail in the Keynesian coffin. The ascendant economists backed him up with models that "proved" that if the interventionists tried to push the unemployment rate below its "natural level"—their actual language—havoc would break loose in the form of upwardly spiraling prices. For the record, those models fit the data for this period and haven't since,[2] but the confluence of stagflation, Reagan, and the rise of the YOYOs put Keynesian economics on the run. (This occurred even though Reagan's "military Keynesianism"—large deficit spending on defense—was a key factor in the economic recovery of the early 1980s.)

The economics that replaced it has had a variety of names. Friedman's variety came to be called *monetarism*, Robert Lucas introduced the term *rational expectations*, but, as noted above, most just call it *neoclassical economics*. There's nothing all that "neo" about it; the "classical" part harks back to some of the early pristine models that were used to prove that the best possible outcomes will prevail for everyone if rational people seek to maximize their own profits, assuming the government generally stays out of the picture.

YOYO POLICIES: MYTHS AND FALSE ASSUMPTIONS

That last part, of course, is relevant to our story. As economic policy has shifted from WITT to YOYO, the perception of government has changed. Under the old policy regime, government was viewed as an ally of the people; in the framework of YOYO economics, it's perceived as a big, stumbling behemoth that can only muck up the neoclassical system, jam the "price signals," and generally stink up the place. Still, even the neo-(e)cons believe there is a role for government. For the die-hards, that role may be reduced to defending the coasts and delivering the mail (and they're not too sure about the mail), but as discussed in chapter 4, there's been no shortage of economic policy ideas from the Bush administration (and no shortage of money, albeit deficit-financed, to pay for them).

To reiterate, the two main roles for government in today's economics are (1) to deregulate in the Coolidge/Reagan "get the government off our backs" sense and (2) to get the incentives right at the individual level. Both of these lead away from WITT, but number 2 is much more subtle than number 1 and thus deserves some explanation. (And as you'll see, numbers 1 and 2 are intimately related.)

Suppose you're the U.S. government operating in the "old school" mode. You worry so much about your citizens losing income from layoffs that you implement a program providing unemployment insurance (taxpayer-financed weekly payments made for a set period or until the worker finds a job). Nice job, Lefty. You've just mucked up some bum's incentive to get a job. Suppose you guarantee a pension. You've blown the individual's incentive to save. What if you tax stock dividend payments or capital gains? You've crimped the incentive to invest. Want to provide universal health care coverage? You'll take away the incentive to conserve (see the "moral hazard" discussion in chapter 1). How about welfare benefits? No. They're a disincentive to work and an incentive to have kids out of wedlock. Do you think it's a good idea to regulate the job market with minimum wages, overtime, and the like? By placing mandates on employers, you're quashing the entrepreneurial spirit.

Sorry, Old School. Your best move is to get with the new thinking and leave well enough alone, even if all doesn't seem so well.

Except that every one of those objections is largely spurious. In my own research, for example, I have found that minimum wages have nothing like the effects their opponents say they do (job losses, firms going out of business, locusts, famine). Solid evidence supports the claim that moderate increases in the minimum wage have their intended effect: they raise the earnings of low-wage workers without hurting their employment prospects. (Other, much more accomplished economists than I have found the same thing.)[3]

Welfare benefits have been found to have very small effects on work and family structure, which is what common sense would dictate.[4] Most people don't base big decisions, like becoming a single mother, on a monthly check averaging a few hundred bucks (which is by no means to say that people think such things through carefully or rationally, just that the welfare benefit isn't a big motivator). Before 1996, when the welfare reform act was passed, welfare recipients worked outside the home less than they would have if they hadn't been on welfare, but just a bit. What blocked them from the job market had much less to do with the stingy welfare benefits and much more to do with the scarcity of decent job opportunities and the lack of government support for those seeking work, like subsidized child and health care. Employment among the poor surged in the mid-1990s because the economy was strong and because welfare reform led to significantly more, not less, government investment in helping poor single mothers find and keep jobs.

And so on. Unemployment insurance may extend the jobless spell a bit, but the effect is tiny and it gives job seekers the opportunity to find better jobs than they otherwise would.[5] The savings disincentive associated with Social Security has never been found to amount to much. As best we can tell, people appear to save pretty much what they would anyway.

So the notion that WITT policies have "unintended consequences" that undermine them is quite bogus. Yet, the YOYOs are incredibly successful with their arguments. Evidence be damned, they'll warn anyone who'll listen that the do-gooders do more harm than good. In virtually every policy debate I've had on these issues, some YOYO will argue that if we raise the minimum wage, we'll get massive layoffs, or that if we try to insulate the unemployed from the hardships associated with a job loss, the next thing you know we'll be looking at a European-style welfare state with French-like levels of laziness and unemployment (Mon Dieu, they've got twenty-five days of mandatory vacation!).

More than once, I've argued with lobbyists for the restaurant industry who claim they're representing the interests of low-wage workers because a minimum wage would price these unwitting victims out of the labor market. From 2001 to 2003, while we were hemorrhaging jobs on a monthly basis, YOYO economists argued that extending unemployment benefits would lead to longer jobless spells—this, during the longest jobless recovery in our history. I recently debated a member of the *Wall Street Journal*'s editorial staff who argued that reducing taxes on the estates of multimillionaires would generate the right incentives for dealing with the aftermath of Hurricane Katrina.[6] You couldn't make this stuff up.

Most members of the media understandably work hard to report both sides of an argument. One could wish they had the time, energy, and incentive to check the empirical findings, like some of those cited above.[7] But as it is, much news coverage of such economic debates quickly devolves to "he said, she said" reports. An important part of the WITT agenda is to be much more effective in setting the record straight with regard to what the evidence shows. The WITTs' lack of success in making their case is a real problem, and one I take up in chapter 4.

The Benefits of WITT, the Costs of YOYO

To be successful, WITTs need to make two points a lot more frequently and clearly. First, policies that pool risk, actively seek full employment, and mandate against undesirable market outcomes don't just generate costs. They also generate benefits and lead us to make critically important investments in ourselves and our society that wouldn't be made under YOYO policies. Second, hyper-individualist policies have some pretty serious unintended consequences of their own.

One tactic of YOYO politics is to disallow discussion of the benefits of WITT policies and to focus on, and hugely inflate, the costs. The alleged inefficiencies associated with Social Security, unemployment insurance, minimum wages, the tax system, welfare, public education, workplace standards, unions, you name it, dominate the economics literature as well as much of the public policy debate. The benefits of these programs get short shrift.

It wasn't until Social Security was under siege that we began to see articles noting that two-thirds of seniors get at least half their income from the program. The introduction of Social Security cut elderly poverty rates in half. And, as Jacob Hacker stresses (and as common sense would suggest), pooling risks can be highly efficient, both in terms of administration and in reduced costs to the individual when risks are spread over more people.[8] The Social Security system sends out checks each month to 40 million people, with administrative costs that amount to a tiny fraction (less than 1 percent) of the total expenditures. Compare this with the much greater costs and challenges of administering millions of individual accounts. The inefficiencies in our health care system are legendary, and they are typically and unfavorably cited in comparisons with the systems of other advanced economies. For example, Canada spends less than a third of what we do on health care administration per capita, yet it insures everyone. In the United States 46 million people are uninsured.

Pooling risks over large populations, and thus distributing the costs of retirement, disability, and illness as broadly as possible, seems intuitively sensible. There are soon to be 300 million of us in this country. Some of us are will be fine; others will get sick. Some will prosper; others will founder. Some of us will get fired; others will be secure in our jobs. Through risk pooling, we distribute these possibilities over hundreds of millions of cases, and life is no longer a lottery where you're on your own to sink or swim. In fact, it's more like a huge group pooling their resources to buy a lottery ticket. True, each person sacrifices the minuscule chance of winning the whole jackpot, but each increases the chance of winning something.

Admittedly, countries with universal health care do more rationing than we do. They spend a smaller share of the resources on the last years of life, and they spend less on the richest clients, who can buy whatever health care they desire. So some people would be worse off than they are currently. But with an equitable distribution of resources, the vast majority would do better.[9]

We simply do not hear enough about when these initiatives go right. There's an ongoing argument about a whether the press suffers from a liberal or a conservative bias, an argument to which I have nothing to add except this: there does seem to be a strange reluctance to point out the upside of governmental market interventions.

When did you last see an article celebrating the benefits to low-wage workers of an increase in the minimum wage, or the costs to them of its long-term deterioration? Welfare reform, which was widely hailed as a success of incentive-based economics, was nothing of the sort. For many poor women, it *was* surprisingly successful, but not because we finally got the incentives right; it was successful because we pooled the risks faced by poor mothers moving into the workplace. We spent more money per welfare case, providing numerous work supports like health care, transportation, and child-care subsidies, plus a significantly expanded tax credit (the Earned Income Tax Credit, which can add upwards of $4,000 to the annual income of a poor family). Even more importantly, fiscal and monetary policy helped move the job market toward full employment for the first time in decades, ensuring ample employment opportunities for low-wage workers.

YOYO economists are so busy wagging the unintended-consequences finger at others that they too often get a free ride on the problems caused by their own approach. Thus, the second point that WITT proponents need to make is that anti-interventionist economics has its own unintended consequences. The Reagan administration's supply-side economists weren't planning for an explosion in government debt, higher poverty rates, and sharply increasing inequality when they pushed tax cuts. But that's what happened.

George W. Bush's economic advisers weren't planning on the

sharpest reversal from surplus to deficit in the history of govern-ment accounts, but that reversal was partially due to their tax cuts (the nonpartisan Congressional Budget Office found the cuts to be the largest single factor explaining the shift). And again, as in the many of the Reagan years, poverty is up and the typical household's real income is down, not to mention the structural budget deficits. Poverty has gone up every year from 2000 through 2004 (the most recent data point as of this writing), adding 5.4 million people, including 1.4 million children, to the rolls of the poor. The typical (median) household income, adjusted for inflation, has been flat or falling for the past five years, the worst period on record.

Tax cuts for the wealthy reliably do only two things: one, they redistribute income upward, and two, they lead rich people to move assets around to take advantage of the timing of the cuts. All the supply-side nonsense about investments, job growth, and higher rev-enue generation is just that: no evidence exists that would be even mildly convincing to an objective person.[10] I'm hard-pressed to think of a more damaging notion than the free-lunch, "tax cuts pay for themselves" silliness that to this day is spouted by those whose real agenda is redistributing wealth upward and blocking the WITT agenda by defunding government programs, or "starving the beast," in YOYO-speak.

For the record, as long as we're talking about unintended conse-quences, the beastie is not starving. Its food source depleted, it lives off debt. The tax cutters didn't count on the Bush administration being one of the biggest spenders to come down the pike in decades. Not that I take any solace in this: the resulting deficits only put off the inevitable—tax increases or spending cuts—until the grown-ups get home. I tackle this interesting conundrum—how is it that this group of YOYOs has increased the size of govern-ment?—in chapter 4.

Whatever the intention, the consequences are the same: poli-cies inspired by YOYO are failing to address our major challenges and are thus failing to truly provide individuals with the platform they need to realize their potential.

"Dangerous for Good or Evil"

It may seem over the top to assert that the shift from one way of thinking about the economy to another way could be as monumentally important as I'm suggesting. Yet, it was Keynes himself who famously recognized that such ideas

> are more powerful than is commonly understood. Indeed, the world is ruled by little else. Practical men, who believe themselves to be quite exempt from any intellectual influences, are usually the slaves of some defunct economist. Madmen in authority, who hear voices in the air, are distilling their frenzy from some academic scribbler of a few years back. . . . Sooner or later, it is ideas, not vested interests, which are dangerous for good or evil.[11]

WITT's political hands are tied by the ideas of many of today's economists and the policy makers they influence. These influential people insist that employment rates and other market conditions are not to be trifled with by some soft-hearted Keynesian dreamer who thinks they can be improved. Moreover, their approach to economic policy provides excessive individualism with a solid foothold. Hyper-individualism is YOYO's foundation, and it blocks the path to a WITT society.

As long as we cannot challenge outcomes like rising poverty amid plenty, middle-income losses, the legions of the uninsured, the vast inequalities shown in figure 1.1, the impact of globalization, the growing insecurities engendered by the risk shifts, the WITT path is blocked. Under the yoke of YOYO economics, you're on your own to triumph or fail. Any intervention would undermine the system.

What's amazing is how pervasive the YOYO way of thinking has become. These days, the difference between a Republican and a Democrat on the economy is that the former believes you should accept market conditions and leave it at that, while the other believes you accept market conditions, but then perhaps repair some of the damage with a sprinkling of redistribution. So, for example, while the Democrats might work to strengthen unemployment insurance, and the Republicans work against it, neither is willing to take the steps to ensure full employment. While Democrats come up with ideas to compensate workers displaced by globalization, they, like their Republican counterparts, hesitate to challenge the doctrine of "free trade" by insisting on enforceable labor and environmental rights, or ensuring that U.S. workers are compensated for the risks inherent in such competition.

As someone whose job is to argue about these issues in the media and in trade journals, take it from me: to argue for interventions that will shape market outcomes and determine at least part of our economic fate is to invoke the wrath of YOYOs. Whether it's recommending steps to ensure full employment, pursue energy independence, suggesting we raise the minimum wage, or promoting a universal approach to health coverage, every case calls forth some variation of the same response: to take any of these steps will cuff the invisible hand and distort the pristine economic system that assures the best possible outcomes for everyone.

Economics, once an elegant and sensible set of ideas and principles devoted to shaping economic outcomes to the betterment of society, has been reduced to a restrictive set of ideology-inspired rules devoted to an explanation of why we cannot take the necessary steps to meet the challenges we face.

Education and Job Training: The Exception That Proves the Rule

One social good, however, is exempt from all this free market ideology, and it is worth deconstructing the one policy area where even YOYOs love to tread: education and training. Whether it's joblessness, stagnating real incomes, globalization, or the offshoring of

American jobs, the go-to solution suggested by policy makers caught in the sway of this thinking is "improving the education and skills of our workforce." This sounds fine, of course, and no one could be against it. But when it stands alone as the only serious solution offered, beware: YOYO is afoot.

While more education is always better, "improving education" as the solution to all of what ails us has become a code for avoiding the steps we need to take to directly address the problem. In far too many cases, it blames the victim, singling out the individual's lack of skill as the reason things haven't worked out for him or her. It removes the responsibility from policy makers and, more pointedly, from the inequities embedded in our market outcomes, as well as in our education system itself, and places it squarely on the ever more risk-burdened individual.

This point cuts to the nub of where we've gone off course. In an economy with staggering new challenges, the current politics and economics place too much of the burden on the individual.

Given the lack of earnings growth over the last few years, for example, many working parents are just making ends meet. Depending on where they live and their family size, they need anywhere from $40,000 to $60,000 to pay for housing, child care, health care, and so on. Child care alone, for a family of four with both parents working, can easily cost $15,000 a year in an expensive coastal city.[12] And these costs are rising quickly. Yet, in recent years the typical (median) household income has declined in real terms, and real hourly wages, the building block of working families' living standards, have been posting historically large losses.[13]

Yet the YOYO agenda would have this working parent manage a private investment account, an unemployment account, and a Health Savings Account while she upgrades her skills enough to compete against workers abroad possessing similar skills but earning third-world wages. We're not quite throwing her to the sharks.

We'll give her a tax break and a voucher for training or health care. But it's up to her to navigate these waters.

There's got to be a better way, one more in sync with the realities faced by most families in the United States today.

But we won't find it in the hyper-individualism of YOYO. The individual stays in the WITT equation, but the new agenda must tap a shared responsibility to create a context for individuals to flourish. Especially now, with the complexities of a modern global economy, the WITT sensibility is as necessary a starting point as it was in the Great Depression.

That may sound peculiar, given that our economy is percolating along just fine. But that's the irony. YOYO-inspired policies have led societies to an incredible juncture where their economies appear to be doing well until you take a closer look at the people in them.

A mantra among economists is that the main determinant of living standards is the rate of productivity growth (that's economic output per hour worked). The assumption is that if we're X percent more productive, we can have X percent more output without working more hours. And between 1947 and 1973, the typical family's income did grow in lockstep with productivity growth: they both doubled. Since then, the typical family's income has grown at about one-third the rate of productivity. With the acceleration of productivity growth since 2000, the gap between that supposedly key determinant of living standards and the incomes of most families has never been wider.

The implications of this split are as staggering as they are underappreciated. Had the median household income continued to grow with productivity, it would now be in the $60,000 range instead of the $40,000 range. As hourly wages fell for many middle-income workers, particularly men, the only way families could get ahead was by working more hours. In fact, families have added over three months of full-time work over the last twenty-five years (that is, they're working that many more hours per year now than they were in the late 1970s). Had wages continued to rise with productivity, they—we—could have avoided that tradeoff and thus had a much better chance of balancing work and family life. The grip of the middle-class squeeze would be far looser in such a world. The angst engendered by trying to pay for housing, health care, and college would fade as the incomes of all families, not just those at the top of the scale, rise with the rest of the economy.

And what about "jobless recoveries"? There's no better phenomenon to illustrate an economy that's leaving many of its constituents behind than an economic recovery without jobs. In both of the last two recoveries, those of the early 1990s and the early 2000s, the economy expanded, but the job market continued to contract. In the most recent case, the recovery began in late 2001, but we kept losing jobs for a year and a half, by far the longest such period on record. Though the job market finally began to expand in mid-2003, the growth was tepid and the labor market remained slack for years. A slack labor market plays a key role in this scenario, because it puts little pressure on employers to bid up the compensation of the workforce, and in this regard, it sets the stage for the gap between productivity and wages to expand (which is why full employment is such a critical plank of the WITT agenda).

Now, here's a fascinating microcosm of the way YOYO creeps onto the scene. In mid-2005, which saw solid economic growth but stagnant wages and incomes for many, all the national polls began to reflect considerable dissatisfaction with the economy. The president and his economic team were forced to take notice and had a highly publicized summer meeting at his Crawford, Texas, ranch. When Treasury Secretary John Snow was asked to comment on the discrepancy between how the economy was growing overall and how people were faring, he declared that it "points you in the direction of greater emphasis on education." His undersecretary, Randal K. Quarles, amplified the point: "If the country as a whole is going to undergo economic growth, then the population has to be able to take advantage of opportunities."[14]

In other words, it's not our fault, it's your fault. The opportunities are there, but you're not skilled enough to take advantage of them. Never mind that the evidence pointed in exactly the other direction. By mid-2005 the only groups to see fairly strong and consistent job growth were those with the lower levels of education. The employment rate, or the share of a given population at work—a proxy for the extent of a group's job opportunities—was up for high school dropouts and down for college graduates. (The reason had much to do with the boom in construction and health services, and the bust in information technology.)

But such facts were not admitted to challenge the hyper-individualistic YOYO analysis, which by definition ignores the possibility of a structural imbalance in the way economic growth is distributed. As is so often the case, the only solution—"Get more education"—handed the problem back to the victim.

Let me repeat what I said before, so as to insulate this argument from specious attacks: more education and more skills are always better, and individuals should always pursue them, both to realize their own potential and to become better informed and more productive citizens. And yes, government has a responsibility to ensure the quality of public schools, as well as to provide access to all who desire a higher education. (Universal access to college for those who can cut it, regardless of their resources, is a policy plank of the WITT agenda.)[15]

But when an economy is failing to produce enough jobs for those at all levels of education, including college graduates, and when it's failing to distribute the fruits of its growth to those in part responsible for the growth—the workers as opposed to the investors—more significant intervention is necessary.

What form should that intervention take? Read on.

CHAPTER THREE

The "All Together Now" Agenda

I RECENTLY made a business trip to Tucson, Arizona, which happens to be where my mother lives in a retirement community. So I schlepped my young daughter along, and we stopped by for a visit. My mother asked if I would speak to her Democratic club, but as my schedule was pretty tight, I declined. She snapped into action and set up the talk, whisking me and the kid, who was assigned to making name tags, over to the community center. (I know, there's deep fodder for psychoanalysis in this paragraph — different book, that.)

It turned out to be a real eye-opener in the following sense: these aging Democrats (my mother is in her eighties) simply do not believe that an economically activist government is a problem. To the contrary, they see the YOYO viewpoint itself as responsible for much of what's gone wrong in the economy. For them, a major problem facing our country is the lack of government effort to correct the challenges I discussed in my talk: globalization, health care, the disconnect between growth and poverty.

I vividly recall their puzzlement as to why government action was so discredited. One man, his face almost contorted with perplexity, asked me, "Why don't more people get that you can't turn to corporations to fix these things?" I explained that distrust of government ran deep these days, which clearly distressed them. As one woman said, "It's not government that's the problem; it's *this* government."

Some in this group were children of the Depression; others were retirees from the factories of the Midwest, where they'd found a solid foothold in the middle class. Their unions fought for secure pensions, which they are enjoying to this day. And here I was, telling them about the aggressive attack on New Deal policies, the defunding of government through regressive tax cuts, the demise of the manufacturing sector, and the fading of union power. They buttonholed me until I left the community center— I still get e-mails from some of them—and while they put it in various ways, they really had one big question: Why isn't the dog barking? Why doesn't a huge majority realize that the only way out of the mess we're in is to rebuild an effective federal government that truly represents the interests of the people?

What a different viewpoint! For it is clearly not shared by most other citizens. Polling data consistently reveal that about half the people in the United States have at least some confidence that government can help solve economic problems, but the other half worry that government intrusion will do more harm than good.

Yet, a central goal of the WITT agenda is to change the political question of our time from, What actions can we take to diminish the role of government in our lives? to, How can we harness the power of government to solve the challenges we face?

Even to me, this sounds a trifle naive. Those poll results are not simply a reflection of some skewed ideology; people have reason to be wary of giving a larger role to government in our economic lives. Even before the government at all levels lethally bungled the response to Hurricane Katrina, a president who constantly promotes his allegiance to smaller government signed a $290 billion transportation bill that originally included the pet project of a highly placed senator, a $220 million bridge in Alaska connecting a town of 14,000 to an island of 50.[1] At the same time, the Congress enacted a bill laden with tax cuts for large energy producers but with no mention of obvious conservation measures like higher auto-mileage requirements or, heaven forfend, higher gas taxes. To the contrary: all of this spending is occurring amid a tax-cutting frenzy.

And those are relatively mild examples of government failure. We spend hundreds of billions on intelligence yet missed 9/11 and got it wrong on weapons of mass destruction in Iraq, in part because our agencies failed to communicate and highly placed officials refused to accept information that didn't match their assumptions. While thousands of our own citizens, along with innocent Iraqis were dying in that misguided war, Congress held a special session to figure out how it could remove the medical treatment of Terri Schiavo, a tragically brain-dead woman, from her doctors.

So, the Tucson Democratic Club aside, it's not surprising that many of us feel a bit defensive advocating government solutions. Even recent presidents, from Reagan to Clinton ("The era of big government is over") to George W. Bush, have inveighed against government.

YOU PAY THE SAME AMOUNT, BUT YOU GET THE GOVERNMENT YOU CHOOSE

The failures of government in recent years pose a major challenge to the WITT agenda. Yet there is a convincing reason to believe that this incompetence can be reversed, and it can be summarized as follows: you don't necessarily get the government you pay for, but you can if you're paying attention.

What this means, as we'll shortly see, is that we've been spending roughly the same share of our economy on the federal government for decades, yet the quality of the service has been, shall we say, a bit choppy. For the same amount of money you can get good government, in the sense of thoughtful leaders earnestly trying to solve the problems we face, or you can get . . . well, let me turn to Hendrik Hertzberg, who puts it like this:

> The reigning conservative ideologues in the White House and on Capitol Hill believe, with apparent sincerity, that the path to economic and social progress for all is to reward—"incentivize"—the rich and to liberate private business from the wealth-destroying fetters of regulation. When these become the highest purposes of public policy, and when the ameliorative functions of government are held in contempt, then a single thread ties together upper-income tax cuts, the dismantling of environmental and safety protections, the shredding of the social safety net, the peopling of regulatory agencies with cronies hostile to their purposes, and, finally, outright corruption. If government is seen as a whore, why not treat her like one? All that remains is to fleece the johns and divide the take.[2]

A touch shrill, perhaps, but there it is: one man's view of what we're getting for our $2.5 trillion investment in the federal government. But our history reveals that such excesses and core incompetence cannot last. Such abuse of power inevitably implodes, and with Iraq, Katrina, the lobbying and warrentless-wiretapping scandals, the deficits, and so on, the fuse may have already been lit. If so, there is an opening for a new set of leaders who, instead of disparaging and exploiting government, truly believe in crafting and implementing a useful agenda.

Here's a picture of what I'm talking about. Figure 3.1 tells the underappreciated story of federal government revenues and spending as a share of the economy: Did spending head south under Reagan, reflecting his desire to dramatically reduce the size of government? How about under the Bushes? There was a notable slide under Clinton, but for the record, that was as much a function of a faster-growing economy as of restrained spending. Under George W. Bush, spending as a share of the economy is back up

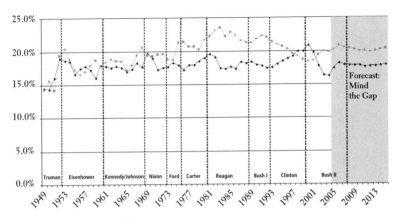

→ Revenues → Spending

FIGURE 3.1

Federal spending and revenues, as percentages of
gross domestic product, 1949–2015.

[SOURCES: 1949–2010: U.S. Office of Management and Budget, *Historical
Tables: Budget of the United States Government, Fiscal Year 2006* (Washington,
DC: U.S. Government Printing Office, 2005), Table 1.3, http://www.whitehouse
.gov/omb/budget/fy2006/pdf/hist.pdf. Forecast: U.S. Congressional Budget
Office, *The Budget and Economic Outlook: Fiscal Years 2007 to 2016*
(Washington, DC: U.S. Government Printing Office, January 2006), chap. 1,
http://www.cbo.gov/ftpdocs/70xx/doc7027/01-26-BudgetOutlook.pdf.]

again. Bush is a hefty spender, though he's more than a bit light
when it comes to paying the costs of the bills he signs.

Our actual spending reflects neither the laissez-faire economics
beloved of YOYOs nor the rhetoric of our leaders. What should we
make of this?

For one, it suggests that we're committed to devoting about 20
percent of the economy to federal spending, which right now
amounts to $2.5 trillion, or around $9,000 per person. Whether the
Democrats or the Republicans are in charge, whether we're in
YOYO or WITT mode, that's what's on the table. In the spirit of
plausibility and sound restraint, any policy agenda should not seek
to change that ratio much, with one exception: to get our health

care system on a rational, sustainable footing, we'll have to expand public spending, but at the same time we'll be able to significantly reduce the amount we spend in the private sector. The efficiencies—that's right, the public-sector efficiencies!—of moving health care coverage from the private to the public tent will enable us to devote less of our economy to health care, as does every other advanced economy in the world (more on this later).

Second, while figure 3.1 shows that deficits are not necessarily that big a deal—we're almost always spending more of the gross domestic product than we're collecting—the projections to 2015 and beyond are worrisome given the recent changes in the tax code and the future expenses associated with our health care entitlement programs (Medicare and Medicaid). The Bush officials are engaged in a scary experiment, spending freely while permanently slashing the revenue base. What's not well known is that even were we to constrain spending—if we froze our spending on things we can freeze (so-called discretionary programs, like student aid, as opposed to entitlements, like Medicare and Social Security)—we'd still be swamped by debt, the accumulation of each year's deficits, within a few decades after the chart ends. Go a bit further, and assume that we significantly reduce the share of the economy that we spend on defense. According to the CBO, in order to meet our entitlement obligations, we're still looking at a level of debt that equals 100 percent of GDP by around 2030 and grows after that.[3]

The decimation of our revenue base is clearly part of the problem, but the far larger part is an unwillingness to plan for the future. Again, we get the government we're willing to accept, and at the behest of the YOYOs in charge, we are essentially being told, "Don't worry, be happy." Cut taxes, raise spending, and pay no attention to that wolf lumbering up to the door.

One could speculate about the YOYOs' motivation. Defunding the government is one way to hamstring it, and this strategy also puts off the day of reckoning until the group that created the problem has left the building. But it seems clear that the ultimate strategy is to force us to significantly shrink the size and functions of government. If tax increases are off the table as the gap between revenues and outlays grows large enough and the debt levels reach our eyeballs (more accurately, our children's eyeballs), we will be forced to cut spending in a big way.

As can be clearly seen from the outcomes of budget battles percolating in late 2005, the initial cuts will predictably fall on the least advantaged (and least politically active), such as those that depend on Medicaid and food stamps. But the budget scissors are reaching up the scale and cutting middle-class programs, such as college aid, too.

Once our debt levels start to spiral, however, our concern over today's cuts will seem like a quaint memory. At that point, we'll be forced to slash away at bedrock social programs, especially health care and pensions. For YOYOs, it is the fail-safe mechanism. The politics of entitlements have thus far prevented them from hacking away at the large WITT programs they've been going after. But if they can stay in control long enough and simply refuse to do anything about the obvious challenges we face, they'll have their way by default.

In that sense, we the electorate are also to blame. It's a lot easier to believe, as Vice President Dick Cheney supposedly believes, that "deficits don't matter" than to figure a way out of this hole. Cheney's admonition is a political, as opposed to an economic, calculation. And it appears to be accurate. In fiscal 2005, for all the YOYO rhetoric espousing the virtues of less government, we enjoyed $320 billion more government than we paid for. A few voices raised points about the stark and simple arithmetic of this arrangement: those who come after us will either have to pay more taxes than we do or have fewer government services. Yet in the absence of a Perot-type scold, politicians are not called to account for such unbalanced ledgers. As they say, "de-Nile ain't just a river."

The WITT agenda takes a very different tack. It recognizes that denial of the realities leads to an unacceptably insecure economic future, without safety nets, without affordable, accessible health care, and without guaranteed pensions. The goal is to work together to first restore faith in government and competency within it, and next to tackle the challenges we face before they tackle us.

THOMAS PAINE: WITT'S FOUNDING FATHER

In any case, we're starting the policy discussion with two realities: nearly all of us are skeptical of government solutions, and except for health care, we can't spend much more than the historical average of around 20 percent of GDP. (We can, of course, significantly alter the composition of the spending package. Do you copy that, Pentagon?)

On the first point—our skepticism or even cynicism regarding government solutions—I once again invoke the spirit of Thomas Paine. As Scott Liell engagingly describes in his book about Paine's transformational pamphlet, many of the major political and social figures of the day were tilted solidly against independence in 1776.[4] True, many viewed the government they had as unrepresentative at best and repressive at worse, but they either could not see outside the box in which the monarchy confined them or felt the time hadn't yet arrived to stage a revolution. Amazingly, in the course of months, and without the help of bloggers, Paine's *Common Sense* changed all that.

For our purposes here, what's important about Paine's work was his framing of the question, What type of government do we want and deserve? Though few articulated more disdain for the state of government affairs (he referred to the king variously as a "wretch," a "tyrant," and a "crowned ruffian"), he clearly and passionately envisioned a far better alternative. *Common Sense* is an angry document, but it's also brimming with the fundamentally optimistic conviction that the colonists could do much better. That it caught on as it did is even more impressive when you consider that monarchical rule was all Paine and the colonists had ever known. Yet his pamphlet moved them to consider a new reality.

Well, all that many in today's polity have ever known is hypocritical rhetoric about the government's inability to get anything right ("hypocritical" in the sense of the spending line in figure 3.1: those who disparage government never do much to reduce it). So those of us who would have it otherwise need to introduce an alternative vision.

Obviously, I recommend a vision in which the pervasive reach and breadth of government helps people come together and build collaborative solutions. Such a vision seems to ask for a leap of faith. After all, why should those who have grown skeptical of government embrace it?

Because there's no "it." The government is not some disembodied beast that we have to live with (or that we can starve). We are our government, or more precisely, it is our expression of our priorities, our concerns, our interconnectedness or lack thereof. Granted, in such divisive times, telling ourselves that we are the government may not move the agenda much past gridlock. But various realities, not the least of which is our lack of preparedness for disasters, natural or otherwise, are already making that gridlock impossible to sustain. We are fast approaching a point where individuals, families, and communities from states both red and blue will be turning to the government for help in meeting the challenges of globalization, retirement, the inequality of economic outcomes, education, job quality, living standards, and so on.

This message came through strongly in a set of focus groups I helped run in the Midwest and South in 2005 on the economic challenges facing middle-income families.[5] The participants, middle-income homeowners with children, were truly ambivalent what role government should take in helping them survive the economic squeeze they all agreed they faced. A solid strain of "It's up to me" came through, both as a deeply rooted value of self-reliance and an expression of their belief that government wouldn't be there for them. (The consensus among these middle-income families was that Democratic administrations give the store away to the undeserving poor, while Republicans give it to the rich.)

Yet another, equally dominant sentiment went the other way. We had to dig for this one, but it was there beneath the surface. It basically came down to "We could use a little help." In one of the cities (Indianapolis), a large corporation (United Airlines) had pulled up stakes a couple of years after the city gave the company millions of taxpayers' dollars in incentives to locate a maintenance center there. At the same time, it laid off hundreds of skilled, well-paid mechanics. As part of its bankruptcy settlement, United also terminated what the mechanics believed were their guaranteed pensions. (One of those guys was my cabbie back to the airport.)

Not surprisingly, members of the focus group viewed this as an unfair outcome that government regulations should have averted. Similarly, they recognized a chasm growing between what they earned and what it cost to send a kid to college. The same with health care. That is, they thought the insurance companies and the HMOs were ripping everyone off with impunity, and they recognized a role for regulation here as well.

How does all this fit into our framework? Obviously, the "bootstraps" strain feeds right into YOYO, which is one reason the YOYO strategy has been so successful. But one message from the focus groups was that we can't pull ourselves up by our bootstraps if you take away our boots. Thus, when YOYO politics doesn't give the broad middle class a fighting chance, there's an opening—I'd argue a pretty wide one—for WITT ideas.

My former mechanic turned cabbie did not want a handout, a tax cut, or an end to foreign trade. He just wanted a chance to fix airplanes. The members of the focus group did not call for universal health care coverage or college-tuition exemptions. But they recognized that government had a legitimate role in clearing the way to a better life. They knew they were playing by the rules and felt that folks like them ought to be able to achieve the hallmarks of a middle-class life: a secure job, reliably good schools, stable health insurance, a chance for their children to go to college. They did not have a sense of entitlement, but they did have a sense of fair play.

For a beltway wonk like myself, the discussions were revealing and important. Those on the project with more focus group experience warned me to be careful not to overinterpret these results. After all, went their caveats, we ultimately spoke with fewer than a hundred people. As an economist with lots of experience crunching data sets with hundreds of thousands of observations, surely I appreciated the risk of extrapolating beyond the sample.

You'd think so. But I'm choosing to ignore their starchy warning and offer this conclusion, because my gut tells me I'm right: people are not nearly as divided along WITT versus YOYO lines as you'd think, given partisan rancor, tight election results, and all that blue-state/red-state stuff. They, and by "they" I mean a majority of the electorate, see a role for both dynamics, and they feel the pendulum has swung too far toward YOYOism. They are thus open to a moderate agenda that provides them with the opportunity to get a fair shake. They'll take it from there.

Granted, years of hearing government being disparaged have taken their toll in terms of a widespread belief that government can help solve problems. But the last few years of YOYO have created a sense that our economic lives have undeservedly become too insecure, and there is thus an opening to introduce a new agenda.

Note the difference between this perspective and that of the Tucson Democrats. The majority of the electorate is not ready to revert to Roosevelt-era interventions. Yet I believe it is becoming undeniably clear to most Americans that the current political situation is leading to deep insecurities, ones that could be avoided if different people were in charge.

All of which means that those interested in building a new agenda have to be strategic about it.

WELCOME TO WITT WORLD

It will take a shift in the public mind-set to build and implement a WITT agenda. This YOYO mess has been decades in the making, and it won't go away unless there's something compelling to replace it, an agenda that convincingly tackles the economic challenges we face.

There are numerous levels to such an agenda. The first step has come be called "framing," which roughly means talking about solutions in a way that resonates with the intended audience. The discussion in chapter 2 about exposing YOYO's faults and making known the benefits of WITT was just such an attempt to frame the central arguments in this book. Once these insights are shared by a majority of the electorate, we can begin to employ politicians that will earnestly strive to serve the majority in meeting the challenges of today and tomorrow. Finally come the steps of constructing, implementing, and evaluating policy changes. (Sounds easy, right?)

Assume that I'm correct and that a majority, maybe a small one but still a majority, is willing to consider a new agenda (and no smart comments about assuming a can opener). What should that agenda look like?

Here, in broad brushstrokes, are some of the ideas that I believe to be consistent with the political philosophy developed in these pages. The intention is not to elaborate on specific legislation in detail, but to sketch out a view of WITT-style policies in a number of critical areas. Yes, the devil's in the details, but the important thing at this stage is not the machinery of all the moving parts or even, beyond a general thematic thrust, the individual policies themselves. What's important is that in each area discussed below there must be a willingness to see the government intervene to shape market outcomes, whether they emanate from next door or Beijing. The fact that YOYO precludes such steps renders it useless in this environment. WITT's inherent activism, its willingness to tackle the problems we face, gives it an upper hand in the marketplace of ideas.

The agenda focuses mainly on three major challenges: globalization, health care, and income inequality. Following these discussions, I offer a few thoughts regarding another important area: education policy.

Globalization

Modern advanced economies are more connected to the rest of the world than ever before. Forty years ago, trade—exports plus imports—amounted to 10 percent of the U.S. economy; now it's 27 percent. Economists swear up and down that this reliance on trade makes us better off than some protectionist alternative, but they are posing a false choice. A continuum lies between the no-borders free trade of the simple economic model (which doesn't exist anywhere) and the sealed-off borders of protectionism. When the global economy calls, you've got to answer, but you can dictate the terms of the conversation.

■ THE PROBLEM While global trade has obvious benefits (more consumer choice, lower prices and interest rates, greater interdependence), its costs are steep and get buried in the cheerleading of public officials and the media. Most notably, our manufacturing sector, a source of high-quality jobs for non-college-educated workers, has been decimated, though not, as is commonly thought, just by an increase in trade. The culprit has been trade *imbalances*: we've been running big deficits in manufactured goods for over a decade, and they've been setting records each quarter.

One result of this record is that the inflation-adjusted median wage for male workers, the hourly pay of the typical guy, was almost exactly the same level in 1973 as in 2005. In real terms (adjusting for price growth), it was $15.76 in 1973 and $15.62 in 2005. This is an amazingly sobering statistic. Over a period when the economy grew by 150 percent, when productivity increased by 80 percent, the typical earnings of male workers went nowhere. Global pressures are by no means the whole story. Research by economist Lawrence Mishel finds that job and wage losses associated with trade explain one-third to one-half the stagnation of men's wages. That's not the whole tamale, but there should be no question that the loss of relatively high-paying manufacturing jobs and the related problems associated with unbalanced trade explain a significant part of that extremely unsettling result.[6]

Globalization helps boost growth through lower prices and lower borrowing costs, but the persistent trade imbalance has had the opposite effect, and that's a key to diagnosing the problem and plotting the solution. Consumption demands that were formerly met with internal production are now met with stuff from abroad, and, unless we replace the lost domestic demand, that saps some of the strength from our economy. That's long been the case in manufactured goods; now that the price of transmitting information across borders is minimal, it's happening in white-collar services as well.

The offshoring of white-collar jobs thus raises the specter that this same fate will spill from manufacturing to high-end services. This is a particularly steep challenge associated with globalization, because the punditry told us for years that if we let the rest of the world do the dirty work, we on this side of the pond could all don downy-white lab coats and point-and-click our way toward a prosperous future. Now we have the Princeton economist Alan

Blinder, a former big shot at the Federal Reserve, predicting that "tens of millions of *additional* workers will start to experience an element of job insecurity that has heretofore been reserved for manufacturing workers." [7]

The YOYO message on globalization is . . . well, it's "You're on your own." Their economists have persuaded policy makers not to mess with the free-trade model lest they thwart the invisible hand that allegedly ensures the best possible market outcomes. So, as noted at the end of the last chapter, you're left once again with "Get more skills." Hey, buddy, if you can't compete with foreign workers, that's your problem, not mine.

■ THE WITT SOLUTION   Start from the proposition that if we're having difficulty competing successfully in international markets, it's a national problem, not that of the individual displaced worker. Simply starting with that frame introduces a level of hope that the YOYOs cannot impart.

But that hope needs to be backed up with concrete action. Under YOYO politics, we've viewed the economy-altering phenomenon of expanding markets with a resigned sense that we have to live with whatever outcomes it yields. YOYO policy makers, with their deference to the investors and lobbyists who benefit most from these arrangements, cannot militate against the downside of globalization, so they must sustain the charade that globalization makes winners of us all.

With a WITT ethos, we're not stuck in that box. We can acknowledge the inevitability of greater trade flows while staunchly resisting the notion that we must passively accept the current outcomes. To the contrary, we must take the gains from trade—and here I will stipulate that the economists are right: such gains exist and they're considerable—and invest them in better opportunities and living standards for those hurt by those arrangements.

When jobs are outsourced, when a factory moves offshore, we

need a safety net for affected workers. The United States has a small program to do this, called Trade Adjustment Assistance, but it is inadequate to the task. Take my word for it (or slog through *The State of Working America, 2004/2005*, which I coauthored):[8] global-ization has had a substantially negative impact on the working lives of millions—recall the flat trend in the median wage for men over the past thirty years. Trade Adjustment Assistance, with outlays of less than $1 billion in recent years, catches hardly anyone in its porous net (for one, it doesn't extend to displaced workers in the service industries, an obvious shortcoming). The safety net should be comprehensive enough to replace lost earnings and maintain health coverage.

The WITT globalization program is not just reactive. It also has a component for stopping the slide of manufacturing jobs. Why are we constantly getting our butts kicked in foreign markets? In part because some other countries don't play fair. The Chinese manip-ulate their currency to keep their exports to us cheap and ours to them more expensive. Many countries with whom we trade have weak or nonexistent labor and environmental standards. With their mantra of nonintervention, YOYO policy makers have to live with this; WITT advocates don't. The United States can play much harder ball with its trade policies. If an evolving economy wants access to our markets, it has to meet some degree of labor standards and honesty in exchange rates.

A much bigger and better proactive idea is to engage in what I call "demand replacement." We need to embark on a large-scale national project that would generate enough demand for goods and services to replace the lost demand embedded in our persistent trade deficits.

The best idea I've seen in this regard is a long-term commit-ment to energy independence. As articulated by the Apollo Alliance, a coalition of unions, environmentalists, businesses, faith groups, and others concerned about our unsustainable energy policies and the loss of well-paying jobs, such a commitment serves many purposes. The coalition argues convincingly that the investment in energy independence has the potential to revitalize and modernize key parts of our industrial base while diminishing our increasingly harmful dependence on foreign oil. The idea is to initiate a large-scale public–private partnership to revitalize the sectors, from manufacturing to information technology, that are reeling from globalization-related insecurities.

The Apollo Alliance cleverly chose its name as a reminder of John F. Kennedy's promise in 1961 that the United States would put a man on the moon within a decade. As it states on its Web site (http://www.apolloalliance.org/), "The technology did not yet exist, but [Kennedy] marshaled the resources of a nation—focusing public investment, research, science and technology education, worker training, and America's industrial might on a common purpose. It was leadership toward a common positive goal and it worked."

Similarly, it strikes me that a large-scale initiative targeted at energy independence could very well lead to an impressive number of moving economic parts that start working together to generate good jobs and lasting innovations.

If, for reasons I'm not considering, energy independence isn't the right pony to bet on, we'll need to come up with another one. For example, it is widely recognized that much of our nation's infrastructure—publicly owned assets ranging from roads, bridges, airports, railroads, trash systems, and ports to public schools and even communication systems—has been neglected over the past few decades. According to the American Society of Civil Engineers, it will take $1.6 trillion to bring our infrastructure up to the standards we need, including $125 billion on schools alone.[9] These systems are obviously integral to our nation's productive capacity as well as our quality of life, but YOYOs since Reagan have ignored them (Clinton was no better on this score). It's a classic market failure: because no private entity can readily profit from such public investments, our public infrastructure will continue to deteriorate in the absence of government investment. A national project to revitalize these critical systems can also be viewed as a great demand-replacement project, paid for in part by the profits from globalization.

The message will be the same: that despite its benefits, globalization has sapped too much demand from vital sectors of our economy, destroying millions of good jobs along the way. This is not a controversial claim. Economists for years have acknowledged the "creative destruction" of such processes, as technology, politics, new markets, and new forms of organizing economic activities generate constant change. Under YOYO regimes, we're helpless to enact corrective policies. It's time to shed those chains.

Health Care

Someone lands here from Mars and asks about the U.S. health care system. You tell the space alien that 46 million people, 16 percent of the population, lack health insurance. The alien thinks that's a little nuts but imagines the system at least saves money. You sheepishly admit that the United States spends more than twice per capita on health care than the average spent per person in other developed countries. The Martian heads back to its ship, figuring there must be a more civilized place to land.

- THE PROBLEM   High costs, inefficiencies, and, most of all, inequities in access and quality—these are the downsides of our health care system. And these problems seem even more stark when we compare the U.S. system to those of the other advanced economies, which spend a much smaller share of their resources on health care yet generally insure all their citizens and have better health outcomes to boot.

Importantly, from a policy perspective, the YOYOs get that we're on an unsustainable path. The most expensive component of a General Motors car is health care for its workers. Without a major change, the unforgiving arithmetic—the fact that health costs continue to outpace economic growth—will hamstring America's competitiveness and seriously damage our economy. So the question is not, will we make changes? but, what kind of changes will we make?

We've already talked about how the YOYOs want to handle this situation: Health Savings Accounts. Turn the problem over to the market, tap individual incentives, yada yada. As one health care expert put it, these accounts move us from "a system where we share risks to one where it's up to individuals to make their own deals and bear their own risks."[10] In other words, pure YOYO.

■ THE WITT SOLUTION Check out this quote from President Bush's chief economist, Ben Bernanke, now the Federal Reserve chairperson: "Importantly, HSAs provide consumers greater incentive and ability to take charge of their own health care."[11]

I think this formulation is a tactical blunder by the YOYOs, who have resisted learning a lesson from their failure to push Social Security "reform." Sure, I'm happy to take charge of my own health, but not my own health *care*! In framing national health care policy, there's tremendous strength in numbers. Even with all the tax incentives in the world, if it's me against the insurers, I lose. Substituting "we" for "me" in that contest leads to a different outcome. Pooling risk by insuring large groups eliminates huge inefficiencies. Insurers no longer spend time and money figuring out which folks need the most health coverage in order to deny them coverage, which is in and of itself a reason for taking health care out of the marketplace. Neither do individuals have to throw the dice with an HSA, betting that they'll stay healthy enough to avoid paying the high deductible and raiding their account.

We're in this together, and we need a plan that explicitly works against the divide-and-conquer tactics of the current system and the HSA "Let's make health consumers smarter shoppers" approach. A system of universal coverage, like that in every other advanced economy, meets this need.

The questions are: what are the specifics? how do we get there? how do we pay for it? and, what do we lose, if anything, by moving to such a system?

It's beyond the scope of this discussion to get into the minutiae of such a system at this stage. And one rule of successful policy making says, don't be in a rush to spell everything out; you'll lose potential constituents before you're off the ground. But I don't want to cop out under a banner of "Assume an excellent, costless plan" either.

Part of what you do in this business is learn as much as you can about proposed solutions and then see what other, smarter people think about them. In this regard, Medicare for All seems like a useful framework. Expanding Medicare, the public coverage program for the elderly, preserves the private system of health care delivery but makes health insurance coverage universal. This is important, because polling data show that most of us are OK with the quality of health care in this country but are increasingly troubled by the lack of affordability and coverage (polls cited in the next chapter also show that support for Medicare is in the stratosphere, at over 90 percent).

As Paul Krugman put it, Medicare for All

> reminds voters that America already has a highly successful,
> popular single-payer program, albeit only for the elderly. It shows
> that we're talking about government insurance, not government-
> provided health care. And it makes it clear that like Medicare (but
> unlike Canada's system), a U.S. national health insurance system
> would allow individuals with the means and inclination to buy
> their own medical care.[12]

You want to talk costs? The advertising, staff, and all the energy that private insurers have to put into hassling you about your claims result in administrative costs of up to about 30 percent of the insurers' total outlays, compared to 2 percent for Medicare. And the situation would be worse under HSAs, because you'd have the added costs of administering the personal accounts. On this point, note that financial market players are champing at the bit for HSAs to take off, hoping to cash in on these fees. It's revealing, for example, that the American Bankers Association is a major player in HSA lobbying coalition. This component of the plan is projected to add billions in HSA administrative costs.

It's estimated that moving to single-payer Medicare for all types of coverage could save upward of $200 billion per year, enough to cover the uninsured. You can quibble about such numbers—could be more, could be less (though most estimates get you to about there)—but be assured: if we moved from the current system to something like universal Medicare, the share of our economy devoted to health care would fall and would start to look more like that of other advanced economies. (The next chapter provides more details about paying for the WITT agenda.)

What do we lose? Since those with the means to do so can still buy their own care, we avoid some of the rationing and triage that other countries, like Canada or the United Kingdom, have instituted. But before any YOYOs get too fired up about the possibility of rationing health care, be aware that tremendous rationing is already deeply embedded in our health care system. It's called *price rationing*, and it's what happens when you try to solve this problem with market solutions like HSAs. If you look at the main way the United States provides health coverage—through the job market—you quickly learn that 20 percent of the people in the bottom fifth of the income scale have health care coverage; in the top fifth, 85 percent of the people are covered through their jobs.[13]

Remember that *New Yorker* piece cited in chapter 1? Writer Malcolm Gladwell begins that critique of Health Savings Accounts with vivid descriptions about the suffering of those among us who are unable to afford coverage. So don't let anyone tell you that Medicare for All will obviously lead to more rationing. Those who now get very little health care will get more; some of those who get a lot may get less (though they'll be free to buy as much as they want outside the system).

Neither am I arguing that moving to universal coverage through expanding Medicare would be costless and painless to all. It's possible that some physicians' salaries will be diminished, since Medicare reimbursement rates can be lower than those of private insurers (physicians salaries are definitely one factor in the wide gap between our spending and that of other advanced economies). Or we could end up with a two-tiered system, where the rich pay for Cadillac care while the rest drive Chevys.

Of course, whenever you bring up the possibility of the government providing universal coverage, some YOYO starts screaming about inefficiencies and fraud. Regarding inefficiencies, as pointed out above, there's just no case on the administrative front; the government program is far more efficient than the private sector in terms of the share of the money flowing into the program spent directly on health care, not on profits, advertising, chasing down insurers, and so on.

The fraud that exists in the Medicare system is partly political. Just as members of Congress add all sorts of baubles to budget bills, so they do the same with Medicare, getting line items in the budget for medical service providers in their districts. But this point just brings us back to the argument for better government (and don't kid yourself: there are lots of palms being greased in the private system too). As I've tried to point out, if you disparage and defund government, you get the predictable result.

It really comes down to this: every reasonable forecast shows that unless we change course, health care costs will swamp the economy, because they are consistently growing faster than GDP. This isn't a public sector problem; the story is just as scary in the private sector. In this regard, the critical question is in which sector, public or private, are we more likely to make the changes that have to be made, including squeezing the inefficiencies out of the system, insuring the uninsured, and redistributing care more evenly throughout society?

As pointed out in the HSA discussion, the YOYOs think individual savings accounts and more head-to-head competition will solve the problem. That approach works wonderfully for millions of commodities in our economy, from pork belly futures to toothpaste at the drugstore. But access to health care is not a commodity; it's a basic human right in an advanced society like ours. So we need to take it out of the market and ensure that it's delivered equitably and efficiently. At least in this regard, we are simply not that different from every other industrialized economy that figured this one out long ago.

Frankly, it's hard to know what will happen when all the moving parts start moving. That's one reason we would want to move slowly, extending Medicare coverage down the age scale in increments. But of this you can be certain: at some point in the next ten to twenty years the United States will be on the path to a very different type of health care. More than in any other policy area, I'm convinced that our health care solution must come from the WITT camp. Markets just can't generate the optimal results, especially regarding equity and efficiency.

Before leaving this discussion, I need to clarify a potential point of confusion. In his second term, George W. Bush and the Congress passed a massive Medicare expansion to pay for prescription drugs. In many ways, the act is a perfect microcosm of all we've discussed thus far (that is, if you can call something that will cost more than a half a trillion dollars over the course of a decade *micro*). In true YOYO fashion—always try to wedge the market in there somewhere—the act does not provide prescription drug insurance through the traditional Medicare program, but insists that such policies must be purchased from HMOs or private insurers (the insurance industry lobbyists liked this part a lot, too). Thus, the act introduced a myriad of plans for seniors to choose from, and most takers found the choices to be overwhelming. (Admit it, do you carefully read the stuff your insurer sends you?) And note again the millions of silos as everyone negotiates a different deal. For prescription drugs, this is just crazy. You're sacrificing the massive bargaining clout that would result from pooling the millions of Medicare participants to negotiate truly deep savings. In fact, in a sop to the drug companies, the act explicitly prohibits such a pool.

And the structure of the coverage is truly wacky. To fully insure people under such an inefficient architecture would lead to drug costs that made even this group blush. So you're covered up to a point, but once you spend too much, you lose coverage. Then you gain it back later.

Finally, when the new law took effect, in January 2006, its implementation was a tremendous debacle (core incompetence reared its head again). Hundreds of thousands of seniors who tried to take advantage of the new system were left off computer listings and unable to get their medications. Governors in numerous states, including Arkansas, California, Illinois, Maine, and Nevada, invoked emergency powers to free up the money needed to repair the damage.

My fear is that such a debacle may besmirch Medicare's good name with a public that has given it stellar approval ratings. Needless to say, this isn't the approach to Medicare expansion I'm recommending. To the contrary, it's what happens when YOYOs resist the efficiencies in universal coverage and risk pooling. They spend hundreds of billions, yet manage to damage the program's reputation.

But don't take my word for it. Don't be moved by the fact that every other country that has thought about health care for more than ten minutes has come to this conclusion. Spend a few minutes Googling *Health Savings Accounts* and *Medicare for All*, and tell me which one looks better.

Income Inequality

Figure 1.1 back on page 31 shows that for U.S. residents, income inequality has risen sharply over the past few decades, reaching peaks unseen since the late 1920s. Since the late 1970s, the real aftertax income of those at the top of the income scale grew by 200 percent, while the income of those in the middle grew 15 percent and those at the bottom 9 percent. Throughout this book I've also alluded to the declines in income and increases in poverty over the past few years.

■ THE PROBLEM According to the U.S. Census Bureau, the real income of the typical household has been flat or has fallen in each of the past five years, the longest such stretch on record going back to the mid-1960s. Meanwhile, productivity growth has been off the charts. In other words, the U.S. pie is growing, but many of those who've had a hand in baking it are getting smaller slices.

That is a major indictment against YOYO economics, and it should provide a huge opening for WITT solutions. Policy makers, citing the truly impressive productivity trend, tirelessly tout the benefits of the new economy, yet many families feel beleaguered, as the costs of housing, health care, and college grow far faster than their incomes.

And this describes only the most recent situation. Figure 3.2 goes back decades to show the growth in productivity and in real compensation—wages plus benefits, inflation-adjusted—of blue-collar workers in manufacturing and of nonmanagers in services. Ranked

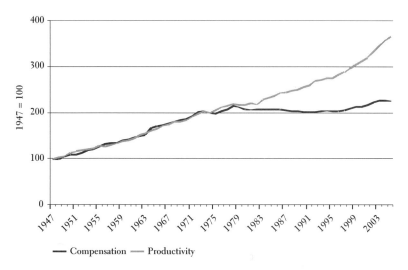

— Compensation — Productivity

FIGURE 3.2

Compensation and productivity of the bottom 80 percent of the U.S. workforce, 1947–2005: Two very different tales.

[SOURCE: Author's analysis of U.S. Bureau of Labor Statistics and U.S. Bureau of Economic Analysis data.]

by earnings, these workers represent roughly the bottom 80 percent of the workforce. That's important, because we're not just talking about burger flippers here. You can be a staff physician at a hospital and be covered in this measure, because you're not a manager.

Now, hourly compensation is the fundamental building block of living standards for working families. All the propaganda about the democratization of the stock market aside, the vast majority of nonretired families depend on earnings, not dividends. True, half of all households hold some stock, but about two-thirds of stock market wealth is held by the top 5 percent of the population. The typical family's holdings are in the fives of thousands, not the tens of millions, and such families' stock holdings are mostly in retirement accounts. The way these families get ahead is to earn more per hour or to work more hours.

For decades, compensation rose in lockstep with productivity. That is, as the workforce became more productive and more efficient, living standards rose accordingly. But starting in the mid-1970s, the compensation of workers began to diverge from their productivity, and that's pretty much been the story ever since, with one important exception: for a few years in the latter 1990s, the two grew at pretty much the same pace. Most recently, the gap has expanded to the widest on record.

Though there have been periods of real income losses, over the long term the *income* of the typical family has not fallen over this divergent period, however. Since the mid-1970s, real median family income is up 22 percent, still not as high as the 80 percent rise in productivity, but not as bad as earnings. How have the American workers done it?

Well, it ain't rocket science. They've—we've—made up the difference by working more. Compared with the previous generation, or compared with those in most other advanced economies, we work our tails off. The typical middle-income married-couple family spends 500 more hours per year in the paid labor market, more than three extra months of full-time work. Most of those extra hours are coming from working wives, and a good chunk of that represents progress in integrating women into the workforce. But it is problematic that families are offsetting stagnant wages and income inequality by working longer.

How do YOYOs respond to these trends? Predictably, with a lot of denial and spinning. As poverty was rising and median incomes were tanking over the past few years, President Bush and his appointees were talking about how great the economy was doing. And if you stick to productivity and other top-line statistics, you can make a case for that. But at some point even these YOYOs had to face the music and acknowledge that some serious living-standard slippage was going on.

As discussed in chapter 2, their solution is more education. And while everyone is better off with more skills, we must go much further if we're to reverse these trends and help people reconnect their fortunes to that of the overall economy. The YOYOs are ideologically unable to take the steps needed to accomplish this. They can only tout the elixirs of globalization, deregulation, and tax cuts while spouting blame-the-victim rhetoric to those of us who just don't have the smarts to grab the brass ring. In other words, there's another opening for changing the way we talk about and approach these economic challenges.

■ THE WITT SOLUTION   If you look closely at that last chart, you'll get an interesting clue about an important component of the WITT solution. Over the latter 1990s, as the job market moved toward the lowest unemployment rates in thirty years—which was about the last time productivity and real compensation rose at a similar pace—the gap between wages and productivity stopped growing. The benefits of full employment, which had eluded us for decades, appeared on the scene for a New York minute, just long enough to remind us of the importance of these conditions. And, so as not to lose sight of the political context, recall that full-employment economics is WITT economics.

By *full employment*, economists are generally talking about a job market where the number of available jobs matches up fairly neatly with the number of job seekers. From the WITT perspective, the key to appreciating full-employment economics is the notion of bargaining power, a factor that gets little play in YOYO economics. It's critical, however, because in periods when workers have little bargaining power, their chances of claiming a fair share of productivity gains are diminished. Thus, a key plank of the WITT platform around the issue of income inequality and living standards is boosting people's ability to get their fair share of economic growth.

Under YOYO politics, your ability to cash in depends on where you're placed in the social and political hierarchy. Some people have corporatist connections (Halliburton has a competitive edge, to put it mildly). And some have wealth connections. When the gap between the rich, the middle, and the poor widens, how you fare depends evermore on what you start out with. And the system feeds on itself, as the hyper-wealthy get the tax breaks and rule changes they seek and hire the lobbyists to keep the money coming.

How can you channel the economy's growth your way under a WITT framework? One way used to be joining a union. The main goal of unions is to boost their members' bargaining power, and their success can be seen in the wage advantage enjoyed by those covered by collective bargaining relative to those (the majority) left out.

But unions have been on the wane for decades, as have related government mandates and corporate norms like the minimum wage or employer-provided health care and pension coverage. One part of the WITT solution is thus to strengthen these mandates and rebuild those norms, but in the absence of such pressures, we need a tight labor market, one where employers are compelled to more broadly share the fruits of productivity growth to keep the workers they need.

If this sounds too simple, consider the evidence for the latter half of the 1990s, which Dean Baker and I discuss in our book, *The Benefits of Full Employment: When Markets Work for People*. The typical worker's wage went literally nowhere over the 1980s, up zero percent, before reversing course and rising smartly in the latter '90s, when the job market tightened. We found what you'd expect to find: full employment is especially beneficial for the least advantaged. You know the adage, when the economy sniffles, the poor catch pneumonia? Well, when the job market gets truly tight, the worst off get the biggest boost.

Between 1995 and 2000, the number of job opportunities grew most quickly for the working poor, and their wages and incomes grew faster than they had since the last time the United States hit full employment, in the 1960s. Poverty rates for African American and Hispanic families fell especially quickly, and at a much faster rate than the poverty rates of white families. Similarly, the share of poor families headed by single mothers declined to its lowest level on record, and it fell much faster than that of married-couple families. For the first time in a generation, the median family incomes of minority families grew faster than those of white families, and the gap between black and white incomes was the narrowest it's been since the Census Bureau began keeping track in 1947.

Remember the statement from head YOYO John Snow (President Bush's treasury secretary) cited in the previous chapter, that if workers only had the skills, they could tap all the great opportunities out there? These same workers—not everyone, but most of them—did great when the job market was really percolating, and their success had nothing to do with skills. Full employment is strong anti-inequality medicine.

So what's the WITT plan to get there? It has two components, the first of which is uncontroversial (or should be); the latter may be a little touchy. The Federal Reserve plays a hugely significant role here, as it has both the official responsibility and the ability to send the unemployment rate heading up or down. (The Fed sets the interest rate that signals investors to speed up or slow down their activities.)

Why, you reasonably ask, wouldn't the Federal Reserve automatically seek to maximize employment? What does YOYO or WITT have to do with any of this? Isn't it axiomatic that the Fed should always be doing what it takes to get us to a tight labor market? Isn't that the point of Keynesian full-employment economics?

Yes, but you will recall that those economics do not rule, and the version that does rule has overseers who worry much more about inflation than about a slack job market, so the Fed in recent decades has tilted against price increases more than it has against sluggish job growth. (To give credit where it's due, Greenspan and company let the unemployment rate in the latter 1990s slide to levels that economists were sure would drive inflation up, but inflation remained quiescent and the benefits of growth began to be shared.) The Fed's actions show a definite class bias, by the way, as the rich are more vulnerable to inflation than unemployment. That's why it drives me a little nuts when the Federal Reserve has ended all its statements in recent years with this phrase: "The Committee will respond to changes in economic prospects as needed to fulfill its obligation to maintain price stability."

Where are those three little words that WITTs long to hear: "to maintain price stability *and full employment*"?

There oughtta be a law. And, in fact, there is, but no one pays much attention to it. The Full Employment and Balanced Growth Act of 1978, which insiders refer to as the Humphrey-Hawkins Act (after its sponsors, senators Hubert Humphrey and Augustus Hawkins) requires the Fed to maintain full employment and even goes so far as to define 4 percent as the unemployment rate consistent with that goal. But parts of the legislation have expired, and for years economists have considered full employment to be closer to 6 percent than 4 percent. That wrongheaded belief is one of the reasons we're in this mess in the first place.

Congress needs to enact a new, pumped-up, muscular version of Humphrey-Hawkins with tough language about full employment. I'd set the rules such that when the unemployment rate rises above 4 percent, the chairperson of the Fed has to go to Capitol Hill and explain to Congress why unemployment has gone above the full employment rate and what the Fed plans to do to correct that serious imbalance.

The government's fiscal policy—tax and spending—is part of the story too. The Congress can and does use policies such as tax cuts and spending increases to boost the demand for workers when the private sector stumbles, a good old Keynesian stimulus.

When all else fails, as Steve Savner and I argue in an *American*

Prospect article, direct public-sector job creation is warranted.[14] This is a tried-and-true way to absorb excess labor supply and provide decent jobs to those stuck in areas with zero labor demand and those blocked by barriers like discrimination. And let's face it, even before Katrina, there was lots of work to be done improving the nation's public infrastructure.

Here again, the specifics are of course important, but the overarching principles are much more so. If the Apollo Alliance is wrongheaded for some reason I don't recognize, or if direct public-sector job creation has destructive unintended consequences, we'll need to find better ideas. The point is, we've got to try. To push back hard against decades of the basic unfairness that falls under the antiseptic rubric "rising inequality," we need to shift some power from the narrow sliver of haves to the big slices of those who have less but who are busy expanding the economic pie.

Along with full employment, unions and higher minimum wages can help too. One of the main reasons for declining union membership lies in power dynamics. The cards are stacked so high against those who try to organize their workplaces that most campaigns never get off the ground. The protections for workplace organizers are toothless, and anti-union employers operate with impunity. There's a neat piece of legislation called the Employee Free Choice Act that would help a lot in this regard. It's another plank in the WITT anti-inequality platform (Google it for yourself and see what you think).

Higher minimum wages are one of the most direct ways to diminish the wage gap between the lowest earners and the rest of the workforce, and it's especially effective for low-wage women workers. But if Congress fails to raise the minimum wage periodically, inflation erodes its value. And in fact, thanks to YOYO inaction on this—Reagan ignored the minimum wage for nine years, and the current Congress and administration are following suit, not raising the minimum since 1997—the buying power of the minimum wage is close to its lowest level in half a century. Had Congress raised it to keep pace with inflation, it would have been around $7.50 in 2005 instead of $5.15, which would have meant almost $5,000 more a year for a full-year worker. That's a huge boost for those living on the edge.

Over the past fifty years, the minimum wage has fallen from about half the average wage to about one-third the average. As the minimum drifts further below the average, workers stuck in minimum-wage jobs end up ever further outside the economic mainstream. It's a classic example of the inequality wedge at work, wherein one disadvantaged group—minimum-wage workers (most of whom are adults whose contributions are important to family income)—gets left behind as the rest of society moves ahead. According to careful economic analysis, that decline in and of itself is partially responsible for the surge in inequality among wage earners.[15]

Another plank for the platform? Absolutely. And it will attract a great deal of support. About one-third of the states, containing about half the labor force, have already taken it upon themselves to enact this piece of the WITT agenda, raising their state minimums above the federal level. A couple of these states are distinctly red, suggesting these ideas resonate across the political spectrum. In the 2004 election, both Florida and Nevada went for Bush and for the minimum wage. The WITT coalition is bigger than you think.

More Planks in the Platform

The WITT platform has many more planks. The three pieces presented here were chosen because they're of central importance but also because they capture the gist of the WITT hopes for a better society. That means using the tools we have at our disposal—Medicare, the minimum wage, Trade Adjustment Assistance, the pro-union Employee Choice legislation—and to expand and strengthen institutions, such as the Federal Reserve, that could much more effectively carry the WITT water to the fire.

I've left out big policy areas under contention, like Social Security and education. The former we have discussed elsewhere. That program is not broken, in the sense that relatively minor tweaks may (or may not) be needed to keep its finances whole decades into the future. Social Security stands as a major WITT triumph, and the YOYOs' attempt to privatize it serves as a motivator for all that's in these pages.

You could write a book on the education-policy war between WITTs and YOYOs.[16] The YOYO strategy—no surprise—is to deregulate the market and spice things up with competition. Their aim is to create the "right" incentives by providing families with vouchers they can use in the private-school market. If that kind of language makes you nervous in this context, join the club.

The WITT perspective, and the dominant law of the land for over a century, is that publicly provided K–12 education, and I'd start with pre-K, is a fundamental right in an advanced society. And while a private market will always exist, primary education is too important to entrust to the marketplace. In fact, the problem with public education harks back to the inequality discussion above: there are public schools in this country you or I would be happy to send our kids to, and others you'd try to avoid at all costs. In other words, education presents another case of highly uneven distribution. Richard Kahlenberg introduces an interesting solution: integrate public education by income level, not by race, to provide low-income children an entrée to better systems and to take advantage of possible peer effects (high-performing students tend to bring up low performers who associate with them).[17]

That's a meritorious idea, but it involves moving kids around—that is, busing them—in ways that have historically been highly problematic. By the time they're ready for school, kids from disadvantaged backgrounds already face higher learning barriers than children from more affluent homes. Fix the distribution of income, wealth, and opportunity, and you'll begin chipping away at other problems too.

Before I close this outline of the WITT platform, it's worth returning to the opening question: given the reputation and performance of the public sector, how can we seriously advocate more government involvement in our economic lives? For the Roosevelt Democrats in the Tucson club I spoke to, that's not a reach. For the rest of us, such advocacy requires a leap of faith.

There are many reasons to take that leap. First, no other institution has the scope to take on the massive challenges posed by health care, globalization, the surge in income inequality, and other issues. Second, we have no choice. The YOYO path is yielding destructive outcomes for too many of us in each of these areas, and we haven't even talked much yet about budget deficits, basic competence (think hurricane relief), and foreign policy. Third, I'm not talking about bigger government. Apart from health care, which we can deliver much more efficiently, we don't need to, nor should we, crank federal outlays much above 20 percent of GDP, the recent historical average. (A brief discussion of the costs of this agenda follows in the next chapter.)

And finally, we need help. Not all of us, and not in some fundamental, life-altering way. In many cases, we just need some equality of opportunity at the start, just a clearing of the way so we can help ourselves. But the message from the focus groups I listened to, a group of folks not champing at the bit for government support, is that most of us need more security in our economic lives. With a strong economy and soaring productivity, we ought to have better access to reliable health care, more confidence in our ability to get our kids to good public schools, and a greater sense that if we play hard by the rules, things will fall our way more often than not.

It's not that much to ask for. But you can't get there on your own.

CHAPTER FOUR

How to Talk to a YOYO

BY NOW YOU'VE learned about YOYOs and WITTs, the policy trends and the policy makers who maintain the status quo, and the broad outlines of the WITT agenda. The agenda makes perfect sense, you acknowledge that its time has come, and if you began this book blind to the faults of YOYOism, the scales have since fallen from your eyes. You're thoroughly committed to the WITT agenda and want to know where you can sign up.

No?

Well, then, let's discuss some objections. I myself can think of many, and I'm sure I'm just scratching the surface.

CAN OUR DIVIDED COUNTRY COME TOGETHER?

One obvious objection is that we appear to be a sharply divided nation, and we're divided along lines that might seem to preclude agreement about the way we should meet the economic challenges of our time. But the key word here is *economic*: we can sustain considerable differences in other areas while we come together on economy policy. The majority of the electorate—the vast majority if we're talking about the potential electorate—has been hurt in one way or another by YOYOism, whether by stagnant living standards, rising economic insecurity, or just plain anxiety about where we're headed. The resounding message from President Bush's recent attempt to privatize Social Security was that most of us are uneasy about the notion that we're on our own. There's no denying that significant splits exist among our electorate, but here's why I believe a WITT agenda can generate enough agreement around economic issues to lead people to put their other differences aside and endorse a new regime.

The insecurities we've been discussing affect most of the people in this country, and the inequalities reach quite high up the income scale. The economy doubled in real terms between 1979 and 2000, while the average real income of those in the middle of the scale rose by 12 percent. For those in the top 1 percent, real income almost tripled, up 184 percent.[1] The most recent data show that only the top 5 percent of households achieved any real income growth in 2004, the third year of a recovery that, according to the YOYO economic cheerleaders, is proof that "the tax cuts are working." So based purely on the increasing reach of economic insecurity, the numbers favor WITT.

And then there are the YOYO policies themselves. If we hang around long enough, we're all going to retire someday, and according to my calculations, only 1 percent of us will make it to the top percentile. So, regardless of our views on abortion, playing the stock market with what would have been a guaranteed pension is something many people of otherwise widely differing opinions oppose. Regardless of our religious or political beliefs, most of us will need health care for ourselves and our families. If we could present people from all walks of political life a choice between Medicare for All and either the current system or, worse, a system of market competition so you can comparison-shop for your health care as you would for tile or insulation, there would be a whole lot of coming together going on.

At least that's what the polling consistently shows. An ABC-

Washington Post poll from 2003 asked a representative sample of Americans which they'd prefer: our current health care system or "a program like Medicare that's run by the government and financed by taxpayers."[2] You'd think that last part about taxpayers would be the coup de grâce, no? That's because the YOYOs have you believing that the mere mention of paying for something leads people to run for the hills. But by almost a 2-to-1 margin (62 percent versus 32 percent), respondents favored Medicare for All. That's not surprising: a 2005 Harris poll showed that favorable opinions about Medicare were astronomically high, with 96 percent either strongly (80 percent) or somewhat strongly (16 percent) in support.[3]

And that wasn't a freak result. The Pew Research Center asked how respondents felt about "the U.S. government guaranteeing health insurance for all citizens, even if it means repealing most of the recent tax cuts."[4] Favoring this proposal, 67 percent; opposing it, 26 percent: over 2.5 to 1. In the 2005 Harris poll just noted, 75 percent favored universal coverage, while 17 percent opposed it, greater than 4 to 1.

You get the same result with Social Security privatization, with a significant majority unwilling to embrace the risk shift.

Similarly, there's no reason to expect that solutions addressing economic inequality will run headlong into a stalemate between blue state and red state. Remember that in 2004, Bush took Nevada and Florida, yet both states passed laws to raise the minimum wage.

Here's an enlightening, though unfortunately rare, example of a YOYO attack that brought together people and their political representatives from all walks of life in opposition. For years, YOYOs have been gunning for the Fair Labor Standards Act, the 1938 legislation that embodies many solid WITT principles, including the minimum wage. The act grew out of the realization that sometimes the job market is so much a "buyer's market" (that is, too many people are chasing too few jobs) that the workers' bargaining power is diminished to the point where they can be exploited. We've discussed the current opposition to increasing the minimum wage. But in 1938, Congress decided that when market forces pushed the wages of the lowest-paid workers to privation levels, it was time to overrule the market by imposing a floor below which it was socially unacceptable for wages to fall.

It was a clear rejection of YOYO economics and, as the Florida and Nevada cases show, a great example of a WITT economic policy that crosses party lines. Support for the minimum wage is typically high, as such things go, with moderate increases usually getting well upwards of 80 percent support. A typical Pew Research Center poll, for example, shows 86 percent approval for raising the minimum from its current level of $5.15 to $6.45, which in polling land means that pretty much everyone agrees. For self-described liberals, support is at 94 percent (no surprise there), but for "social conservatives" it is 79 percent, a resounding majority.[5]

My belief that some economic policy issues cross the usual battle lines was bolstered by an argument regarding another Fair Labor Standards Act protection, a debate in which I was intimately involved. In their first term, the Bush folks went after overtime regulations, the rule that hourly workers get time and a half pay for work beyond forty hours per week. It turns out that overtime earnings are an important part of the income of millions of working families, and these earnings have become even more important as real wages have stagnated over the past few decades.

The administration officials argued that they were modernizing and streamlining the law, but it looked to me and others that they were just following the risk-shifting, deregulatory playbook. My colleague Ross Eisenbrey and I found, for example, that the Labor Department had seriously low-balled the number of people at risk for losing the right to overtime pay. Other researchers picked up on the issue, and a healthy national debate ensued.

Now, here's the kicker with regard to the magnitude of the potential WITT constituency. Not only was there a significant public outcry against the proposed change, but enough people also went to their representatives that the Congress — and we're talking about a group dominated by a significant conservative majority — voted not once, but twice, to block the new rule. But since the president can execute this type of change regardless of the Congress's wishes, the YOYOs in the executive branch couldn't pass up the chance to take a whack at this basic worker protection.

The rule thus became law, and after such long odds had been surmounted to get the Congress to vote against it, that was pretty discouraging. On the other hand, the outpouring of public sentiment on behalf of protecting the right to overtime pay revealed a potentially important, if largely untapped, willingness to fight back. The administration's next big policy thrust on economic (in)security was Social Security privatization, and when that hit the skids, its failure reinforced the idea that a majority of the population was beginning to say, "Enough already with the risk shifting."

Is Something the Matter with Kansas?

The episode concerning the change in overtime regulations suggests that there exists a sizable constituency open to both the YOYO critique and the WITT agenda. But I'm also aware of *What's the Matter with Kansas?*

The latter is an interesting read by political scientist Thomas Frank, who examines the phenomenon of people who seem to vote against their economic interests to support their religious or cultural ones. Frank argues that the Right has done a great job of getting significant swaths of the electorate to support candidates who endorse conservative values even though the candidates' economic platforms will cost such voters dearly and directly. It's the old "Pay no attention to the YOYO behind the curtain" routine.

Frank may have overstated the case, however. In my analysis of the 2004 presidential election, I found that economic problems such as weak job creation and sliding living standards heavily benefited Kerry, especially among low-income voters.[6] In other words, significant numbers voted their pocketbooks and wallets. Similar points are elaborated in a recent academic study by a political scientist who takes a close look at the validity of Frank's hypothesis.[7] According to that study, voting patterns reveal that working-class people from Kansas and elsewhere continue to be swayed more by bread-and-butter economic issues than by social issues. This has been the trend for decades and was especially the case in 2004.

WITT's *Appeal to the Kansan in All of Us*

Still, Frank is on to something that poses a challenge for WITTs. People sometimes do vote against their economic interests, for all kinds of reasons. But to the extent that these voters under the spell of misleading YOYO arguments, I believe their views can be changed, because of the simple uniting, fundamental truth that we are all in this together. The concept that members of our society should fairly share both its risks and resources, especially when through their contribution to our nation's productivity, they are responsible for creating those resources, is especially powerful and comforting in a world generating ever higher levels of economic insecurity. It is even more powerful and comforting when the party in charge is exacerbating those insecurities by pushing YOYO policies. If the WITT agenda can be tapped, it can cut across lines that sharply divide people on noneconomic issues. I'd even go further and suggest that the agenda can unite partisans on those issues as well.

But to reach those whose orientation would not normally lead them to embrace WITT politics, a bold platform must be raised to stand in stark contrast to that of the YOYOs. I outlined the overarching themes in the previous chapter, but they need to be framed in such a way as to resonate with folks like those in the Indianapolis focus group and in Frank's book. Recall that in the focus group discussions, individualistic sentiments about picking oneself up by one's bootstraps coexisted with the desire that government would prevent corporate power from running amok and would help clear the way for the average guy or gal to get a fair shake. Recent polling and election outcomes clearly suggest that people across the United States are angry about losing overtime protections, uninterested in playing the stock market with their Social Security savings, ready to support universal health coverage and a higher minimum wage, and increasingly unsettled by the insecurities engendered by incompetent governance.

THE OPTIMISM OF WITT, THE PESSIMISM OF YOYO, AND SOME ADVICE FROM TOM PAINE

The pollsters say you've got to offer an optimistic message, and they're right. You can't win converts by constantly squawking about the shortcomings of the other side while neglecting to state clearly and simply what you stand for. The YOYOs have maintained the charade of a positive agenda with a clever framing of the "opportunity society," but as I've tried to describe in these pages, it is a wolf in sheep's clothing. YOYOs can tell you why we can't build a secure pension system, expand and strengthen the safety net, offer a universal-coverage health care program, or begin a national push toward energy independence. Yet WITT proponents have plans for all of the above.

The irony is that the YOYO agenda is a much more pessimistic one. But you can't fool all the people all the time. When the pendulum swings back, the WITT agenda will have the numbers to be enacted.

Still, what about the damn-the-torpedoes, single-issue, I-don't-care-if-we-offshore-every-job-in-America-as-long-as-we-outlaw-abortions voter? He or she is probably out of reach. But even here, I wonder if some part of the WITT spirit could reach through what seems like an impermeable barrier. I hear this approach in the recent rhetoric of Hillary Clinton, who talks about reaching out to the antichoice crowd to discuss ways to avoid unwanted pregnancies.

The idea is to find pragmatic ways to lower the heat on the most divisive issues, thus freeing up the political space to pursue commonalities. While this approach won't work with immoderates, surely there are those on both sides of the abortion or religion wars, for example, who have had it with business as usual and are willing to work together to reduce the number of unwanted pregnancies or reduce the decibels of the "intelligent design" debate. For some voters, *moral values* is code for condemning homosexuals, which takes those voters off the WITT reservation. But pollsters say that for others, *moral values* means "personal integrity, family solidarity, and the social compact," the latter in particular being very much in the WITT camp.[8] These nuances offer potent examples of how we might break down barriers that divide us on economic issues.

Once again, we can turn to Thomas Paine for advice. He faced a similar challenge in trying to unite a populace that was, according to historian Scott Liell, politically, culturally, and economically fragmented. What's more, the British "relied upon the colonies' different, sometimes competing, cultural, political, and economic interests to keep them fragmented."[9]

Paine's solution was to find the thread that united the colonists' grievances and to use the flashpoint arguments of *Common Sense* to tie that thread to the British monarchy. The thread he found was dependence on the throne, and his pamphlet is largely an explanation of how that dependency was enslaving the colonists, "tracing almost every evil in colonial society back to what he saw as the root evil of British rule."[10]

The thread today is, of course, the risk shift, the pessimistic "You're on your own" admonition of the YOYOs regarding the challenges at the root of economic insecurity in America. Though their differences then were as pronounced as any today, the New England fisherman and the Southern planter were united in their support for Paine's arguments.

Similarly, when the conversation in the focus groups my colleagues and I ran turned to health care, job security, or the ability to pay for their kids' college, I saw people with very different cultural and political values acknowledge that the current system was failing. The same cross-cutting levels of support are evident in the debates about the minimum wage and overtime. What's more, you don't get poll results in the 70, 80, and even 90 percent range unless there's widespread agreement among diverse populations. What's missing is an agenda around which these different people can unite. In the 1770s, it was the independence movement. In the 2000s, it's the WITT agenda.

NEWS FLASH: YOYOS ARE NOT FISCAL CONSERVATIVES

For all their "small government" rhetoric, the YOYOs are big spenders. The Clinton administration spent at a rate of 1.5 percent per year, compared to 5 percent for the current Bush administration. (Reagan came in at 3 percent per year; George H. W. Bush at 2 percent.) Perhaps you think that the comparison is unfair because George W. Bush is paying for a war (though I can see lots of reasons for charging him for this one) and for entitlement programs like Social Security that are driven by an aging population, not his spending decisions. But the same differences arise if you look only at so-called discretionary, nondefense spending (George W. Bush: 5.9 percent, Clinton, 2.4 percent). In fact, Bush II ties that poverty warrior LBJ on this measure.[11] Of course, this administration does stand out from the rest in that it doesn't bother to pay the bills.

This is a group that's engaged in shifting economic risks off government, so what's with the big-ticket spending? The administration passed a Medicare expansion that it sold to Congress on the basis of a ten-year price tag of $400 billion, now thought to cost around $540 billion. Similarly, a new transportation bill came across the scanner with a price tag of about $290 billion. The wars in Iraq and Afghanistan cost in the range of $80 billion per year (up to $350 billion and counting),[12] and rebuilding the Gulf Coast after Katrina is expected to amount to $150–$200 billion over five years. Admittedly, this doesn't look like a YOYO agenda.

Proving the point, some bona fide conservatives are expressing their deep dismay. Listen, for example, to Bruce Bartlett, a veteran economist of the Reagan and Bush I administrations, inveighing against the profligate ways of his party:

> I used to believe that the Republican Party was the party of small government. That's why I became a Republican. I don't believe that the federal government has the right to one penny more than absolutely necessary to fulfill its essential functions as spelled out in the Constitution. I think government is over-intrusive and could do what it has to do far more efficiently and at lower cost, which means with lower taxes. Therefore, it bothers me a great deal when Republicans initiate new entitlement programs, massively expand pork-barrel spending, and show the most callous disregard for fiscal integrity.[13]

How is it that these administration guys talk YOYO but spend so much? It's pure politics. Rest assured, the Bush team got the "starve the beast" memo about cutting government programs; they just didn't read the whole thing. They mastered the part about cutting taxes, but their political strategy has thus far precluded cuts in spending, and with their Republican allies controlling both houses of Congress, they haven't been able to say no to their friends and funders when it comes to handing out the goods. As George Packer put it, the Bush administration is "not anti-government, just anti-good-government."[14]

Let's be very clear: none of this heavy spending gets us any closer to the WITT agenda, which, as I've stressed, is not about growing the size of government (though it sure ain't about shrinking it either). To the contrary, unless we change the debate, the "beast" starvers will prevail and we'll be on our own whether we like it or not. As noted in the previous chapter, given the gap between share of the economy we're collecting in federal tax revenues and our spending obligations, particularly on health care entitlements, something's gotta give.

The arithmetic is simple: you either cut spending or get revenue collection back on its historical track, hovering around 20 percent of GDP. And here's where YOYOism fits in. While the Bush team hasn't had the courage of its convictions to hack away at the spending side of the ledger, the YOYO philosophy absolutely dictates that when it comes to cutting spending or raising revenue, you cut and run. All this risk shifting and privatization implies that we solve the problem one way, and one way only: by shrinking government.[15]

So, yes, I recognize that the YOYOs holding the purse strings aren't gutting the government in a way that's consistent with their philosophy or rhetoric. But the combination of their fiscal policy— all those tax cuts—and their commitment to shrinking government while shifting risks to individuals means that unless we change course, spending cuts will come. Such cuts will start—in fact, with the 2006 fiscal year budget, they have started—with the low-hanging fruit: the social safety-net programs like Medicaid, welfare, job training, student loans, and food stamps that have neither a powerful political constituency nor a bevy of K Street lobbyists. But the big bucks do not reside within these so-called domestic discretionary programs. If we fail to address the coming fiscal debt burden, the big cuts will have to come from the entitlement programs, especially Medicare. At that point, the idea of tapping government to help meet the challenges of globalization, health care, income inequality, and so on will seem like a quaint memory once held by a naive group of dreamers.

IF THE WITT AGENDA IS SO GREAT,
WHY DON'T OUR LEADERS SEE IT?

More than a few people are talking about this stuff in one way or another. Most are among the punditry (Paul Krugman at the *New York Times*, E. J. Dionne at the *Washington Post*, Peter Gosselin at the *Los Angeles Times*, Jacob Hacker at Yale University). Precious few politicians are talking about the WITT agenda, but here too are exceptions, and they're pretty damn exciting. I cheer them on in the concluding chapter.

Still, if the WITT message is as potentially powerful and unifying as I'm suggesting, shouldn't some visible politician have stumbled on it? If a majority in the electorate needs to hear a different vision articulated, wouldn't the party out of power be responding to that need? To the contrary, it seems that many in the Democratic Party have been busy trying to craft some sort of YOYO-lite, consciously running away from a more interventionist platform. What's up with that?

I can think of two reasons, both misguided, why these politicians have avoided the WITT path laid out by myself and others. But before I explore them, note that whatever the politicians are doing, it's not working. As G.W. Bush's second term unfolded, the YOYO agenda started to look pretty tattered, and the larger Republican agenda appeared to be in trouble, possibly in deep trouble. Key conservative leaders and their allies were under indictment, Iraq was becoming a weighty political albatross, the Katrina debacle wouldn't go away, and the president's approval rating was tanking and taking the party down with it.

Yet the same polls revealed that the Democrats were failing to catch a lift from any of the Republican negatives. Now, it's reckless to riff too far off some weekly polling results, but the Democrats' lack of success seems to stem from one fundamental reason: you can't fight something with nothing. And "nothing" here includes any watered-down version of your opponents' agenda in hopes of picking off their supporters.

Under certain circumstances, a party out of power can claim to be the "party of change" and run on a platform of "we're not them." But the stars have to align just so for that to work, and it's no way to run a party.

The Pervasiveness of the YOYO Ethos

One reason WITT hasn't surfaced much is because of the incredibly pervasive reach of contemporary "here's why you can't do that" economics, as described in chapter 2. In that discussion, I noted that in today's economic policy debates, far too often the sole difference between a Democrat and a Republican is that the former is willing to consider some sort of posttax redistribution of our national resources to help the disadvantaged. When it comes to big WITT ideas, like serious public investment in energy independence, or Medicare for All, or commanding the Federal Reserve to elevate full employment as a primary goal, both sides wilt. They've both bought into the notion that you can't nudge the invisible hand of market forces and have thus cordoned off the very place we need them to go.

This will change as today's economics yields to that of tomorrow. While we can't know what it will look like, I'm optimistic that it will by necessity be much less focused on individual incentives and much more on fully utilizing our collective potential. It will have to be, in order to clean up the fiscal mess—the unsustainable deficits, at both the federal and the international levels—and to more effectively shape the outcomes of globalization that today's economics insist we must passively accept.

Soon, the non-college-educated, displaced blue-collar workers won't be the only ones unreceptive to the global cheerleaders.

They will be joined by the white-collar stalwarts of both parties, who will want to know what their elected officials plan to do to help them deal with offshore competition. At some point, voters will recognize that the "get more skills" advice of neoclassical economics, its only response to foreign competition, is inadequate, and they will insist that their leaders come up with something more, something beyond blame-the-victim rhetoric. I have suggested that through a national endeavor toward energy independence or a significant rebuilding of our public infrastructure, we take steps to recreate the demand for labor, both white- and blue-collar, that globalization has sapped. But the larger point is that "the times, they are a-changin'," and the thrust of economic analysis will change with them. Perhaps the changing of the intellectual guard, the ascendancy of WITT economics, will free up some policy makers to embrace this more activist path.

Spooked by Populism

Another reason we don't see the WITT agenda surface in a big way is that important players in the Democratic Party, particularly centrists and "third-wayers," sometimes conflate the progressive agenda I've tried to articulate in these pages with a populist agenda that might alienate the cautious sliver in the middle of the electorate that decides elections these days. The political strategy of these folks — the Democrat Leadership Council, for example, but you could also view aspects of the unsuccessful Kerry campaign in this light — has been to be just a little bit less YOYO than their opponents and to hope that this enables them to peel away just enough moderate voters to get over the top.

The problem is, this strategy usually doesn't work. It alienates the base, and most voters can sniff out the difference between a true believer and a poseur who's trying to jockey for position ever so slightly to the left.

The fear is that the types of ideas outlined in the previous chapter signal an abandonment of the cautious middle ground in favor of a populist agenda, that is, one that pits the common people against the elite, labor against capital, Marx against Adam Smith . . . you get the picture. But the WITT agenda is as much old-school progressive as new school: think TR (Teddy Roosevelt, a competent Republican) meets FDR. The hallmark is an amply funded, competent, not too big government that undertakes measured interventions to help its citizens better cope with the challenges they face.

I'm not trying to be cute. Nationalizing health insurance, raising the minimum wage, preserving Social Security—these are obviously key planks of the liberal platform. And given that all the breaks have fallen to the elites over the past few decades, we could use a good dose of populism to balance things out. But full employment, energy independence, a sane fiscal policy, and a responsible government able to rise to the challenges faced by its citizens, from hurricanes to globalization—these policies reside under no ideological roof. No one has a monopoly on economic security. These ideas do not pit groups against each other, except perhaps YOYOs against the rest of us, and as I've stressed, there are a lot more of us.

So once political actors are freed from the bonds of the rigid economic scolds and the unfounded fear of populism, look for WITT ideas to be much more visible. In fact, in the concluding chapter, I quote liberally from the recent writings of a couple of politicians who get this stuff, including centrists like Tom Vilsack, the chair of the aggressively centrist Democratic Leadership Council. The centrists' espousal of WITT rhetoric is a hopeful sign that they recognize the importance of drawing clear distinctions between their agenda and that of the YOYOs.

You Forgot to Mention This Little Matter of the War on Terror

Washington pundits tend to be a little like the drunk in the Gary Larson cartoon. He's standing at a bar shouting at a kangaroo, "Let me tell you a little something about marsupials!" That is, regardless of background, we feel we can hold forth on everything under the sun. Whatever expertise I can claim is in economic and social policy, and I want to try to avoid that particular pitfall, so I hesitate to offer much detail here, particularly regarding the best strategy for dealing with this threat.

However, one highly relevant point should be considered regarding the general thesis about YOYO versus WITT. Common sense and our experience to date strongly suggest that as far as feeling more secure goes, "You're on your own" is no better a basis for foreign policy than it is for economic policy. From an international perspective, our standing and power seem diminished both by government incompetence vis-à-vis Iraq (the absence of weapons of mass destruction, the horrors of Abu Ghraib, the lack of a postwar agenda) and by government arrogance vis-à-vis our partners, whom we signaled, with great machismo, that consulting with them would compromise our independence. As the terrorist attacks in England and the rest of Europe have shown, in a global sense, we, the vast majority of the world community, are in this together. Yet the view of some potential allies that we are a rogue elephant on the world stage undercuts our efforts to effectively work together to contain the terrorist threat.

Then there's the issue of core competency. The YOYOs, with their emphasis on shrinking government and shifting risk, have hollowed out the competent core of the agencies created to get a job done. The president appoints cronies to key security positions and congratulates them their performance even when they've obviously failed. Combine that dynamic with a lack of accountability, and it's no wonder many citizens feel that this regime is not up to the task of dealing effectively with terrorism. Having seen how the Federal Emergency Management Agency responded to the Gulf Coast hurricane — and FEMA is an agency embedded in the Homeland Security Administration — few of us feel more secure.

This perception does not depend on our politics, either. New York mayor Fiorella LaGuardia once commented that there's no Republican or Democratic way to clean the streets; there's only the right way. I don't claim to know the right way to combat zealots who want to kill innocents. But I believe most of us want our leaders to think in pragmatic, nonideological terms about the best way to infiltrate terrorist cells, to coordinate agency actions, and to set up response systems that inspire faith and a feeling of security in the citizenry. We also recognize that when irresponsible tax cuts starve the government of the revenue it needs to ensure preparedness, we all suffer. In sum, when it comes to fighting terror, we want and need good government and fiscal discipline. That's not the YOYOs' strong suit.

This WITT Stuff Is Going to Cost a Fortune

No, it won't. As I've said all along, we can implement many key elements of the WITT plan, the types of things discussed in the previous chapter, without raising the federal share of GDP beyond its historical level of around 20 percent. We do have to raise revenue from its current 17 percent to come back in line with this, so it's good-bye, tax cuts. Which is just to say we've got to obey the written law. These cuts are all set to expire within the next ten years, so let 'em sunset and let's then get to work on the WITT agenda.

A side-by-side comparison of costs is not possible, because the WITT/YOYO debate is not simply a matter of this policy versus that one. It's a debate about the government's role in our lives, about pushing against the surge in risk shifting and the resultant economic inequality, about eschewing the hyper-individualism that blocks our willingness to pool risk. It's a debate about whether we can work together to meet our economic challenges with an activist agenda that shapes outcomes instead of rolling over before them. You can't really put a price tag on a political philosophy.

But it would be a cop-out not to try. This is especially true because, despite their performance of the past few years, YOYOs favor less government. If true YOYOs were in charge, instead of these pseudo-types spouting YOYO rhetoric while spending without regard for the consequences, we'd already see a smaller share of GDP spent by the government. So I want to be clear: the WITT agenda is more expensive than the true YOYO agenda. However, with the exception of health care, it doesn't call for spending a much larger share of our GDP than we do now (and combining private and public expenditures, the health care share needn't grow much, either). Moreover, the living standards of most Americans will be a lot higher under WITT politics than under YOYO. If we do it right, we can get what we pay for.

If the YOYOs prevail, many more tax cuts will be enacted in the coming years. Even as we are coping with the aftermath of the Katrina disaster and paying for the ongoing wars in Iraq and Afghanistan, YOYO constituents are lining up at the Bush administration's ATM for a $70 billion cut in taxes on capital gains and dividends. We should restore most of those cuts and use that revenue to tamp down the fiscal hemorrhage and implement the WITT agenda.

Here is the gist of how we could fund WITT programs. You pay for the work of the Apollo Alliance, or some similar large-scale, demand-inducing, energy-independence or infrastructure project by taking back the Bush tax cuts. Even just the high-end cuts would yield about 2 percent of GDP per year (including interest payments you wouldn't have to make on the debt incurred).

But spending all that on the big demand-side project might put us right back in the land of structural budget deficits (the type you can't grow your way out of). We want to avoid that, so we'd probably have to make incremental investments and watch what happens. If a successful large-scale program leads to faster growth and boosts federal revenue, the gains can be invested in deficit reduction and reinvested in energy independence.

Full employment, another key plank in the platform, is also growth enhancing and more than pays for itself. For every point less of unemployment, government revenue rises about a half a percentage point of GDP. That's one of the main ways the budget swung into surplus in the Clinton years. A higher minimum wage is costless from a budgeting perspective; its impact is largely to redistribute income from profits to low-wage workers.

Which leave us with paying for Medicare for All.

As I've been careful to point out along the way, universal Medicare will bring the WITT programs to over 20 percent of GDP, but there's no question that the nation will save big, maybe upwards of $200 billion per year, enough to cover all the uninsured. The savings result from the much lower administrative costs and the absence of profits in the universal coverage program.

Now, here's the beauty part: by shifting expenditures from the less efficient private sector to the more efficient public sector, we can provide more coverage yet spend no more as a nation than we're already spending on health care. Employers pay close to half a trillion dollars per year to purchase private insurance for their workers, and it's clearly a competitive burden, especially for manufacturers (think auto producers) who have to compete against those (think the Japanese) who don't have this albatross around their necks. (The Japanese spent 8 percent of their GDP on health care in 2002 compared to our 15 percent, and they had far better outcomes in both life expectancy and infant mortality.) As Representative Dennis Kucinich, an advocate for WITT in general and universal Medicare in particular, said, "We're already paying for universal coverage. We're just not getting it. We're pouring a large portion of every health care dollar into the waste of the private insurance companies, their executive salaries and stock options, their lobbying and advertising."

Again, as stressed in the previous chapter, though I'm convinced that valuable efficiency gains are to be had with Medicare for All, I'm not advertising a free lunch. Some will do worse under a system of universal coverage, a system that will inevitably ration some aspects of care that now flow freely to the well-insured. But others who suffer from the plague of "price rationing"—those who can't afford either coverage or care—will do better. For the vast majority in the middle, if consumer satisfaction with the current Medicare system is any guide (and I'm of course not talking about the recent debacle of the Bush prescription drug bill; see what happens when YOYOs leave their playbook?), we should be fine with the change.

To ensure that we start out in a way that does not lead to a sharp increase in the combined public and private share of GDP devoted to health care, I'd set up Medicare for All so that any taxes we levy on employers to pay for the universal coverage would roughly equal the premiums they're paying now (or should be paying) on their private plans. That is, an employer that pays 15 percent of its payroll to private insurers for health care would keep paying that share. But the dollars would flow to an expanded Medicare program that reached beyond the elderly.

It is difficult for some people to hear *efficiency* and *government* in the same sentence, and even harder to imagine that a federal agency could beat the private sector in this particularly critical area. But, as I stressed earlier, that perception is the result of decades of government bashing, in both rhetoric and action. It's absolutely the case that you can create a wasteful, inefficient government if you staff it with incompetent cronies, run it according to edicts from lobbyists, and gut its revenues while you're at it. But the luxury of disparaging and beggaring government is no longer an option.

And even with all this bashing and defunding, the federal government provides insurance far more efficiently, in terms of the number of people covered per dollar, than the private sector. When health insurance coverage is taken out of the market, and risks are pooled instead of carried by individuals, some very impressive savings begin to materialize.

Another resource to tap for the WITT agenda is the defense budget, which has risen 50 percent since 2000; the United States is spending 1 to 2 percent more of GDP on military stuff than in 2000. This is obviously related to the war on terror, most prominently the wars in Iraq and Afghanistan. Presumably, these wars will not last forever, but regardless of the outcome, defense experts have identified significant waste. Lawrence Korb, Reagan's assistant secretary of defense and a guy with major street cred on this issue, writes that we could save $60 billion per year by eliminating antiquated but ongoing weapons programs.[16] Note that spending these resources on the WITT agenda means a shift in the composition of government spending, not an increase.

NOW, WE NEED A MOVEMENT

So that's the framework of the WITT agenda. I'm not saying the agenda is costless, especially compared to the YOYO agenda. But neither am I waving my hands and assuming away the price tag. We should have a rough sense of the costs on the table, but let's put them right next to the benefits. When we do so, we learn two things. First, the costs are well within the range of our historical spending, and second, the programs may repair a lot of the damage the YOYOs have done and may forestall more destruction down the road.

The YOYO critique, the WITT rationale and agenda, a few considerations of where the latter might not be so convincing—

those were the easy parts of this discussion. Now comes the hard part. How do we build a movement like this to fruition? Scribbling down ideas is no biggie. Framing them in the most effective way is a bit more challenging, but there's an industry for that. The challenge is to find the time, energy, and people to build the movement and move the agenda. The concluding chapter speaks to that prodigious challenge.

It Takes a Movement

MY MIND IS spinning as the wheels of the plane lift off the Heathrow runway. True, I've never resolved my jet lag since landing here a mere few days ago, but that just explains part of my agitation. For I've seen a society embrace the WITT agenda, and it was good.

A WITT DEMO MODEL

In late 2005, a study group from the United States, of which I was a member, visited the United Kingdom to learn about its initiative to end child poverty by 2020. In turns out that a couple of years after he was elected in 1997, Prime Minister Tony Blair gave a speech wherein, out of nowhere, he declared this goal. It took the government officials in the relevant agencies by surprise, they told us, but they rolled up their sleeves and got to work on it.

Members of Parliament and the Blair government built, and continue to build, a comprehensive system designed to boost the incomes of working poor parents, mainly through subsidies to low-wage earners. They raised the minimum wage and continued to push it up yearly. They built a system to help single mothers get access to affordable, high-quality child care (to make it easier for them to hold down a job), and they instituted programs to develop healthy and school-ready preschoolers, teens, and young adults. They launched a cabinet-level government agency, the Social Exclusion Unit, to deal with the combination of problems that interact to keep families poor: a lack of marketable skills, chronic unemployment, poor housing in high-crime areas, and so on.

There have been hiccups getting the many pieces of this puzzle to work together—getting the right tax credits to the right workers hasn't always gone smoothly—but the British are making progress: child poverty is down significantly in the United Kingdom since the latter 1990s, and the new initiatives are clearly playing an important role in this decline. (On our side of the pond, the child poverty rate was higher in 2004 than in 1999.)

We wondered what had motivated them to take this on. It turns out that in the mid-'90s, members of the Labour government, nudged by sympathetic academics and advocates, recognized that income inequality had risen unabated for fifteen years—a period when the British were pursuing their own YOYO agenda under Margaret Thatcher. Their child poverty rates were the highest in Europe. (Here again, the evidence is incredibly consistent: the outcome of the YOYO-inspired policy set is not the widely advertised better macroeconomic performance; the outcome is a lot more inequality.) Many in the policy-making and academic communities were disturbed by this record, but more than that, they were deeply concerned about the future social and economic risks inherent in there being such a large number of materially deprived children. As their treasury secretary, Gordon Brown, put it, "Children are 20 percent of our population, but 100 percent of our future."

To me, these programs looked like an All Together Now demo model. Without any clear conception of how, or even whether, they could accomplish it, members of the Labour government undertook to fundamentally change the economic trajectory of millions of their fellow citizens. It's quite bold when you stop to think about it: elected officials in a major advanced economy decided to try to do something about a trend they viewed as unjust and ultimately harmful to the prospects of their society. (Although when you put it that way, isn't that what governments are supposed to be doing?) Despite the admonitions of YOYO economists that investing a couple percent of GDP on the initiative to end child poverty was incompatible with globalization, they are going ahead with it, and the results are generally impressive. Child poverty is falling and the economy remains solid. The YOYO predictions that a higher minimum wage would kill job opportunities have (once again) been proved wrong.

I asked one politician if he worried that the policies they were implementing were incompatible with global competition. To the contrary, he said. "How can the UK compete globally if a third of our children grow up poor?"

What if you don't end child poverty by the targeted date of 2020? we asked. The question didn't really interest them. The target, they argued, focused the minds of the politicians, the agencies, the tax-payers. Without it, they would not have gotten as far as they had, and if they failed to hit it, they'd try to figure out where they went wrong and try something else.

GETTING THE AGENDA OFF THE PAGE

Could it happen here? Could we make a commitment of this magnitude, not necessarily to eliminate child poverty (though the full-employment agenda would surely help achieve this goal), but to universalize health care, or achieve energy independence, or put an end to our own inexorable rise in inequality?

Obviously, I believe we bloody well can (sorry, I'm still over UK airspace). We have in the past, and the time is nigh to try again.

The challenge is to get the WITT agenda off the page and into the public conversation. That will require a clear message, skilled messengers, and a willingness among the public, if not an insistence, that we begin to make the vision real. Before the American Revolution, Thomas Paine's *Common Sense* churned up a groundswell of support for independence that provided our founders with the support they had been waiting for to break from the Crown. This same interaction between bottom-up energy and top-down leadership helped fuel the civil rights movement. To what extent are the pieces in place in our country for a WITT revolution?

The message is in place, and messengers are on the horizon. The last part, a groundswell of support from the grass roots—well, that's not quite here yet. Its absence is what stands between YOYO and WITT, between an economically unbalanced society and one in which growth is broadly and fairly shared.

THE MESSAGE

We're heading down the wrong path, and look where it's gotten us so far. We're fiscally bankrupt, we're less prepared to deal with disasters than we were before 9/11, and while millions of working families see the insecurities of the global economy, too few see the benefits. Even while the U.S. economy posts impressive growth rates, middle-class families feel squeezed, and with good reason. The typical household's real income fell each year from 1999 to 2004, the worst stretch on record. The productivity of the nation's workforce rose 3 percent in 2005, yet real wages fell for the bottom 95 percent of wage earners, meaning we're working harder and smarter yet falling behind. We're worried about the quality of our kids' schools, rising college tuition, and access to health care.

If you're not one of the chosen few—those who craft the trade deals, those for whom estate tax cuts are passed—your government is not working with you to meet these challenges. And even if you have all the tax breaks and private accounts in the world, you can neither fight the sources of insecurity alone, nor can you ensure a reliable pension or health care security for yourself. You cannot "embrace globalization" on your own. None of us, standing alone, handcuffed by the policy makers who argue that any tinkering with the market will kill the golden goose, can bring about economic justice. We can only passively watch the economic elites and their lobbyists steamroll our dreams for a better life for ourselves and our kids.

All together now, left and right, red staters and blue, let us reject this vision.

Together, as a society of groups with acknowledged differences, we need to rebuild economic security from the ground up. We no more have to uncritically accept the economic conditions we face than the British had to accept the highest child-poverty rates in Europe, or for that matter, than Paine's countrymen had to accept the British. We can construct the economy that serves us best, one that maintains its potential growth yet distributes its fruits far more broadly than today's version. We already have many good ideas, big and small, for recreating a sense of economic security and remastering our economic fate. But to get to these ideas, we have to be willing to entertain a new vision.

In this vision, government is a tool to meet great challenges. Only the national government has the scope to reverse the risk shift and undertake risk sharing, in the name of both efficiency and equity. It's not a vision of more government. For the sake of continuity, efficiency, and political viability, we ought to devote about the same share of the economy to government as has been the historical norm: about 20 percent of GDP, with one exception. By universalizing health insurance coverage, the share will rise, but the decline in private-sector resources devoted to health coverage will more than offset the increase.

Some will view harnessing government to realize the WITT agenda as an impossible goal, given the corruption at the highest levels. But today's feckless government is the inevitable result of decades of defunding programs, along with the trash-talking, crony-ism, and cynicism of those in charge. Under the YOYOs' watch, the system has devolved to a point where it serves a contracting cir-cle of those whose contributions provide them with access. How else can you explain proposals in a post-Katrina environment to cut spending on health coverage for the poor and on job-training pro-grams for the less skilled at the same time that calls are made to end the tax on the estates of multimillionaires?

But this dysfunction can be reversed. Our government is ours. We can debase it and discredit it, or we can reclaim it, restore it, and build it back up to a point where it can fulfill its intended purpose.

While this book has largely stressed the importance of reforming federal economic policy, that's just a means to an end. The ulti-mate goal is a society characterized by economic fairness, one where your chances of a good life are not wholly a function of your position in the income scale. The goal is to reconnect the living standards of working families to productivity, to use our tremen-dous national wealth to ensure universal health coverage, to meet the globalization challenge by reducing economic insecurities.

We've tried the YOYO approach and it has not worked. It's WITT's turn now.

THE MESSENGERS

OK, but where are those who might lead the WITT movement?

Truth be told, it's too early to say. The polls consistently—not this week up, next week down, but as a solid trend—show dissatis-faction with where the leadership has been taking us, particularly on the economy. One can confidently assert that a majority of the U.S. population is open to envisioning a path closer to WITT than to YOYO. Think back to the points made in chapter 1 regarding the failure of the Bush administration to sell Social Security privatization, or the lack of resonance of its message "We're going to let you take control of your health care coverage." People correctly view this risk shift as a daunting, unwelcome proposition, but don't have a countervailing vision to replace it.

It so happens that a few notable politicians are poised to promote that vision. I cite two here because they've written about it in ways that quite directly capture the spirit of the All Together Now movement.

Barack Obama is the extremely popular junior senator from Illinois. He's obviously eloquent, but more importantly from my perspective, one can find in his rhetoric a call for recalibrating much of what goes on in government. He's careful not to lose sight of the individualist impulse, but he's mindful of its limits, and he's refreshingly clear about how the YOYOs have hijacked the individualist thread to unravel our social fabric.

He expresses these views especially clearly in a commencement speech he gave at Knox College in Illinois—a must-read from the nascent WITT canon. Rather than try to summarize his truly inspiring words, allow me to quote liberally. In this excerpt, he hits back hard against the YOYOs' risk shift in the face of global competition:

> Like so much of the American story, once again, we face a choice. Once again, there are those who believe that there isn't much we can do about this as a nation. That the best idea is to give everyone one big refund on their government—divvy it up by individual portions, in the form of tax breaks, hand it out, and encourage everyone to use their share to go buy their own health care, their own retirement plan, their own child care, their own education, and so on.
>
> In Washington, they call this the Ownership Society. But in our past there has been another term for it—Social Darwinism—every man or woman for him or herself. It's a tempting idea, because it doesn't require much thought or ingenuity. It allows us to say that those whose health care or tuition may rise faster than they can afford—tough luck. . . . But there is a problem. It won't work.[1]

Our economic success, he goes on, has always "depended on a belief in the free market; but it has also depended on our sense of mutual regard for each other, the idea that everybody has a stake in the country, that *we're all in it together* and everybody's got a shot at opportunity."

OK, I added the italics in a none too subtle effort to connect his message to mine, but it wasn't a reach. Obama casts YOYO as Social Darwinism, and as such, a betrayal of what has historically made us great and broadly prosperous. He also stresses the hopeful core of WITT by recognizing that we have a choice. That is, we don't have to adjust ourselves to the current conditions as if they were immutable. That's an essential feature of WITT reasoning. The YOYOs' position is that we have no choice, which is why we must accept the risk shift, the insecurities, and the greater inequalities that accompany their agenda.

The WITT message is far more hopeful, and this is a critically important selling point.

Tom Vilsack, the governor of Iowa, also stressed these themes in a 2005 speech.[2] Vilsack, who was on John Kerry's short list for the vice presidency in 2004, chairs the centrist Democratic Leadership Committee. I'm not privy to any inside information, but it seems clear that he harbors presidential aspirations.

Vilsack expounds on many of the themes noted above. For example, he accuses the Bush administration of accepting the upside of globablization while providing "no strategy for dealing with its downside." The key here is his acknowledgment that globalization has a downside, something YOYOs cannot admit, and that the government must craft a strategy to offset it.

But it was the lessons that Vilsack took from Hurricane Katrina that really caught my eye. He begins an article in *Blueprint Magazine* by stating that the tragedy of Katrina reminds us that we are "a national community, and not simply a collection of disconnected individuals or groups," and continues:

But at the same time, the storm's aftermath showed that our national community has been diminished by the inadequate and sometimes incompetent response of one of its essential elements, our national government.

Let me be clear: Government alone is not the embodiment of our sense of community; but you cannot have a strong, united, and effective community without it. *Government is nothing more nor less than the instrument whereby our people come together to undertake collectively the responsibilities we cannot discharge alone. . . .*

These observations are not obvious to many in power in Washington today. The failures in our national response to Hurricane Katrina did not simply stem from the mistakes of individuals whose replacement would take care of the problem in the future. *These failures represent an ideology of contempt for the responsibilities of government, and for the sense of community that is fundamental to self government.*[3] (Italics added)

As I've said throughout, our government is ours. With Katrina, we have most recently seen the lethal results of the ideological path he describes. But you can see variations on the same theme in the deterioration of the situation in Iraq, the inept implementation of the Medicare prescription drug program, and the most recent lobbying scandal to rock the Congress. And Vilsack makes clear another central point: it's not just the present team of YOYOs leading us down this destructive path. His message, in this article and others, is that our failure to meet the challenges we face is the absolutely predictable outcome of decades of anti-government ideology.

In the midst of a political discourse that has been so divisive and pessimistic, I find this rhetoric extremely hopeful, and I believe that if Vilsack gets the visibility he deserves, others will find it hopeful as well. It's pure WITT thinking, and he, like Obama, opens up a broad political space for actively meeting the challenges we face, a space cordoned off by the YOYOs and their "don't go there" economic police force.

In fact, I encourage you to spend a few minutes perusing the

Web sites of these men and reading their speeches. Both of these politicians recall historic victories that have come about when political actions were directed toward the common good, from taming the robber barons to winning world wars, legislating civil rights, and giving voice to workers through building the labor movement. The achievements they invoke, the vision they espouse, are diametrically opposed to the risk-shifting, "no can do" spirit of the YOYOs faced with the challenges of the era. By reminding us of how we acted together in the past to overcome challenges to our freedom and our security, Obama, Vilsack, and others evoke the liberating possibility that we can once again do so.

These men operate on the stage of national politics while others act on the state level in ways that also inspire hope. The Economic Analysis and Research Network (see http://www.earncentral.org/) is a network of dozens of state and local research and advocacy organizations (my EPI colleagues and I work closely with the EARN groups). The groups in this network are actively pursuing pieces of the WITT agenda in their states, including higher minimum wages and health coverage for the underinsured, while seeking to protect state budgets and generally push back subnational YOYOs.

Then there's ACORN (the Association for Community Organizing and Reform Now) and the Industrial Areas Foundation, two groups with hundreds of thousands of members. ACORN has been a major player in getting cities to adopt living-wage laws and most recently has helped the victims of Katrina get back on their feet. Both ACORN and the IAF reach far into the ethnic minority, immigrant, and religious communities. They're tremendously energetic, creative, and effective.

You thought that college students were only interested in iPods? The Roosevelt Institution is a network of think tanks, run and staffed by college students, that formed after Kerry's loss in 2004. Many of these student activists wanted to keep working toward improving government policies and to do so in a way that tapped the tremendous resources at their disposal, including sympathetic faculty members. By 2005, they had chapters in about thirty colleges and universities.

I could go on for a while here citing small, feisty groups engaged in some aspect of the WITT agenda. The point is that there's a buzz on this WITT-versus-YOYO stuff. You may have to strain a bit to hear it, but I can confidently assert that the message is being broadcast by messengers of varying ages across widely scattered areas.

What about the people?

A RETURN TO COMMON SENSE

"We have it in our power to begin the world over again."

So wrote Thomas Paine 230 years ago, in the conclusion to *Common Sense*. We too have it in our power to change our world, and we can do so with nary a musket shot.

Paine was well aware of the challenge of a new vision. Updating his words slightly: "I know it is difficult to get over local or long standing prejudices, yet if we will suffer ourselves to examine the component parts of the [YOYO agenda], we shall find them to be the base remains of . . . ancient tyrannies [unsuited to meet the challenges we face]."

The YOYOs are in decline. The results of their leadership are simply becoming unacceptable to too many of us, the risk shifts too severe and insecurity inducing. The question is: are there enough of us to make the leap to the activist WITT agenda?

If my analysis is right, a majority of Americans want to fill the political space being opened by the ideas of Barack Obama, Tom Vilsack, and other leaders like John Edwards, who has been talking WITT since he entered politics.[4] And that's because it's a more secure space.

For that to happen, the proponents of WITT need to communicate their positive vision and contrast it with the restrictive vision of YOYO. They must be willing to play the instrument Vilsack describes, a government where people come together to face the challenges of the new economy. And their selling point must be the economic security of WITT relative to the insecurity of YOYO.

WITT supporters understand and applaud globalization, but instead of casting our citizens out into the global marketplace to fight it out with each other, and with the Chinese, the Indians, and all other comers, they want a plan. That plan reinvests globalization's dividends in a large-scale program that replaces the demand for labor, a program such as energy independence. If it works, the benefits will be more and better jobs for both blue- and white-collar workers. If not, we try something else.

WITT supporters want to live in a society where the benefits of growth flow to all of those responsible for that growth. That means the living standards of working families become a central concern of central bankers: Main Street gets the same attention as Wall Street. As a full-employment program helps our living standards reconnect with productivity, as incomes grow through higher hourly wages, not just more hours of work, the stresses of balancing work and family will be reduced.

Neither our families nor our firms can prosper in a world with so much insecurity around health care. The waste and irrationalities in our current system, public and private, are unsustainable. Other advanced economies have solved this challenge by universal health care coverage, an idea whose time has come. This change by itself will reduce the economic insecurity of millions of families.

This could take a while. It could, for example, take years to restore enough faith in government for the majority of our citizens to appreciate that while the private market will always be at the heart of wealth generation, it's the purview of the federal government, not the market economy, to get us out of the YOYO box.

While I believe that the candidates we elect in the coming years will be of a different cast than the risk shifters now in charge, it may take a while for them to repair the damage that has been done, both in a spiritual sense (restoring trust in government) and a structural sense (restoring fiscal sanity and putting competent people back in charge, not just at the top of the ticket, but all the way down the line).

If it does take years to find the path away from YOYO and toward WITT, let us not be discouraged. As Paine himself put it, "'Tis not the concern of a day, a year, or an age; posterity are virtually involved in the contest, and will be more or less affected, even to the end of time, by the proceedings now."

And though Paine said it regarding the cause of independence, common sense dictates that "the sun never shined on a cause of greater worth" than coming together in the interest of building a fair economy.

Do YOYO Policies Yield Better Economic Outcomes?

AS THE INDICATORS in appendix table 1.1 show, periods when YOYO policies were in ascendance are not associated with better economic outcomes. To the contrary, during the periods when such policies were most aggressively pursued—the administrations of Ronald Reagan and George W. Bush—the results were generally the least impressive, especially for the typical family's income.

The table shows the annualized growth rates of variables in the U.S. economy over (mostly) ten-year periods, with two intervals broken out for special comparison. The years chosen generally represent peaks in the economic business cycles, as defined by the National Bureau of Economic Analysis (a swinging set of dudes who determine the dates when recessions and recoveries take place). By comparing business-cycle peaks, economists implicitly control for the impact of the cycle itself on these measures, making these comparisons more appropriate than ones taken over presidential terms.

Following the war effort, taxes came down in the 1950s, and growth was quite robust. However, this was no YOYO period. Policy makers pushed some massive redistributive programs, such as the GI Bill, and the social safety net was expanded. Regarding economic policy, Keynesian demand management (see chapter 2) was coming of age; note the very low average unemployment rate and

APPENDIX TABLE 1.1

Annual changes in key economic variables, 1949–2005

Years	GDP	Employ-ment	Productivity Growth	Real Invest-ment	Median Family Income	Unemployment Rate	
						Average over Period	Change per Year
1949–1959	4.1%	2.0%	2.7%	3.2%	3.6%	4.6%	–0.04
1959–1969	4.4%	2.8%	2.7%	7.0%	3.4%	4.8%	–0.20
1969–1979	3.2%	2.5%	1.9%	5.3%	1.3%	6.0%	+0.23
1979–1989	3.0%	1.8%	1.4%	3.1%	0.6%	7.1%	–0.05
(1984–1989)*	3.7%	2.7%	1.5%	2.8%	1.9%	6.5%	–0.44
1989–2000	3.1%	1.8%	2.0%	6.9%	0.9%	5.6%	–0.12
(1995–2000)†	4.1%	2.4%	2.5%	10.1%	2.2%	4.8%	–0.32
2000–2005	2.7%	0.3%	3.3%	0.9%	–0.7%	5.2%	+0.22

* The Reagan boom
† The Clinton boom

NOTE: All dollar changes are inflation-adjusted.

TABLE SOURCES:
GDP: U.S. Bureau of Economic Analysis, NIPA table 1.1.6, "Real Gross Domestic Product, Chained Dollars," http://www.bea.gov/bea/dn/nipaweb/TableView.asp?SelectedTable =6&FirstYear=2003&LastYear=2005&Freq=Qtr.
Employment: U.S. Bureau of Labor Statistics, *Current Employment Statistics*, http://www.bls.gov/ces/home.htm.
Productivity: U.S. Bureau of Labor Statistics, *Productivity and Costs*, http://www.bls.gov/lpc/home.htm.
Real investment: U.S. Bureau of Economic Analysis, NIPA tables 5.3.5 and 5.3.4 (deflator), http://www.bea.gov/bea/dn/nipaweb/SelectTable.asp?Selected=N.
Median family income: U.S. Census Bureau, Historical Income Tables, http://www.census.gov/hhes/www/income/histinc/f05.html.
Unemployment rate: U.S. Bureau of Labor Statistics, *Current Population Survey*, http://www.bls.gov/cps/home.htm.

the historically strong growth in median family income. This strategy continued throughout the 1960s. As the text notes, demand managers became quite emboldened, calibrating growth with tax cuts and hikes to meet the booms and busts of the business cycle. It worked, too, as the growth in median family income growth actually exceeded the growth in productivity, a sign that income inequality was falling. The bakers of the economic growth were clearly getting bigger slices of the pie.

As chapter 2 describes, the 1970s were a transitional period, and with the 1980s you hit Reaganomics and the first bit of evidence that something is amiss. The supply-side tax cuts were supposed to give rich people an incentive to crank up their investments, leading to faster growth that would trickle down to the rest of us. But the rate of real investment slowed to the lowest in the table (excepting the Bush II years), and as for trickle down, fuggedaboudit. Employment growth was OK, though slower than the 1950s and '60s, but the typical family's income grew only 0.6 percent per year in real terms: "bupkiss," as my grandma would have said. Family income grew less than half the rate of productivity, a clear sign of the inequality of the era.

The Clinton years provide another view of how the YOYOs have it wrong. The Clinton tax changes generally raised taxes on higher-income families and lowered them significantly on those at the low end. Did investment crash and burn as a result? Did productivity and job growth grind to a halt, impoverishing the middle class? To the contrary. Especially once the full program took hold, investment boomed and productivity sped up, as did job growth.

For a microcosm of WITT versus YOYO tax policies, compare the two five-year periods of the Reagan and Clinton booms. (I'm not implying that Clinton embraced the WITT agenda, but I am comparing two regimes that broadly reflect the differences between WITT and YOYO.) Reagan did better on job growth, though both periods were solid here. But the inequality, high unemployment, and worse productivity outcomes of the 1984-89 period led to worse results for the living standards of middle and low-income families, compared to those of the full employment period: 1995-2000. With the help of the low average unemployment rate of 4.8 percent and productivity growth of 2.5 percent per year (a point faster than that of the Reagan boom), median family income finally took off. Poverty rates (not shown) also fell more quickly in these years, down 2.5 points, 1995-2000 compared to 1.6 points, 1984-89 (so much for "trickle down"). Moreover, the seemingly inexorable growth in inequality was arrested.

It soon broke out of jail. The Bush II years stand out as uniformly lousy except for productivity growth (and don't think that Bush is at a disadvantage because he hasn't had a 10-year span yet; as shown by economist Lee Price, in any reasonable comparison, the Bush economic record is weak).[1] The YOYO regime of Bush II, and I'm thinking especially of supply-side tax cuts for the rich, ends up posting the worse results in the table. It should be a stake through the heart of "trickle down" policies: investment tanked to the lowest level on record, as did jobs, and family income fell in real terms despite impressive productivity growth, implying that a powerful wedge of inequality was channeling income growth upward.

Bush II is presiding over fast productivity growth, but the important point to recognize is that this growth is in no way related to the chain of events specified by supply-side economics, which operates through more investment and greater labor supply. The productivity boom in these years is due to (1) the ongoing impact of information technology that began to goose productivity growth in the 1990s and (2) fewer jobs. By definition, a growth in output with a decline in jobs equals faster productivity (productivity is defined as output per hour).

As I said in the main text, I don't consider the discussion in this appendix a slam-dunk case against YOYOnomics. It's not a detailed economic analysis that controls for all the other factors driving all the variables (I've reviewed that evidence too, and there's not much support for YOYO initiatives there either).[2] But these simple, descriptive results should be enough to put the burden of proof solidly with those who want to argue that cutting government revenues is the pathway to growth.

INTRODUCTION

1. See John M. Broder, "Voters Showed Less Appetite for Tax Cuts," *New York Times*, November 15, 2005, final edition A-1, http://select.nytimes.com/gst/abstract.html?res=F30711FD3B5A0C768DDDA80994DD404482.

CHAPTER ONE

1. Cited in Harold Myerson, "The Stuff-Happens Presidency," *Washington Post*, op-ed page, September 7, 2005.

2. Paul Krugman, "Killed by Contempt," *New York Times*, sec. A, September 5, 2005, http://select.nytimes.com/gst/abstract.html?res=F50B17FC3E550C768CDDA00894DD404482.

3. Elkan Abramowitz, Letter to the Editor, *New York Times*, sec. A, September 9, 2005, http://select.nytimes.com/gst/abstract.html?res=F50E14FD38550C7A8CDDA00894DD404482.

4. Alyson Metzger, Letter to the Editor, *New York Times*, sec. A, September 9, 2005, http://query.nytimes.com/gst/fullpage.html?res=9807E5DC1331F93AA3575AC0A9639C8B63.

5. See, for example, David Brooks, "Katrina's Silver Lining," *New York Times*, sec. A, September 8, 2005, http://select.nytimes.com/gst/abstract.html?res=FA0C16FA39550C7B8CDDA00894DD404482.

6. Interestingly, one of the tough challenges the reformers face is how the government can pay Social Security benefits to today's retirees if payroll taxes are diverted into private accounts. Answer: It can't. (Implications of answer: huge debt buildup.)

7. Robert J. Shiller, "The Life-Cycle Personal Accounts Proposal for Social Security: A Review," working paper 11300 (Cambridge, MA: National Bureau of Economic Research, May 2005).

8. Syl Schieber, director of research for Watson Wyatt Worldwide, quoted in Mary Williams Walsh, "Many Companies Ending Promises for Retirement," *New York Times*, January 9, 2006, A-1, http://www .nytimes.com/2006/01/09/business/09pension.html?ex=1294462800& amp;en=bd0ead34db40bf98&ei=5090&partner= rssuserland&emc=rss.

9. By the way, that hybrid I mentioned brought up another objection from the YOYOs. Early on in the Social Security debate, some analysts suggested a way to keep the program "spiritually" intact yet introduce the earning power of the stock market: Instead of requiring the govern-ment to build its funds in the bond market, it could invest in the stock market too. That is, the government could add stocks to its portfolio and disseminate the earnings among Social Security recipients. But the privatizers would have none of this. They argued it smacked of gov-ernment ownership of private capital, though I suspect a bigger prob-lem for them was that it lost the millions of small-investor silos of the privatized program—the "You're on your own" part.

10. Malcolm Gladwell, "The Moral Hazard Myth," *The New Yorker*, August 29, 2005, http://www.newyorker.com/printables/ fact/050829fa_fact.

11. See Paul Fronstin and Sara R. Collins, *Early Experience with High-Deductible and Consumer-Driven Health Plans: Findings from the EBRI/ Commonwealth Fund Consumerism in Health Care Survey*, EPI/CEPR issue brief 205 (Washington, DC: Economic Policy Institute, December 2005), http://www.ebri.org/pdf/briefspdf/ EBRI_IB_12-2005.pdf.

12. George W. Bush, in a question-and-answer period after a speech delivered January 19, 2006, in Sterling, Virginia, http://www .whitehouse.gov/news/releases/2006/01/20060119-2.html.

13. The evidence is that unemployment insurance enables them to take an extra week or two; as I show later, research suggests recipients use this time to seek better jobs.

14. The reversal at the end of the figure reflects the bursting of the stock

market and tech bubbles in 2000. Though these numbers stop in 2002, other sources suggest that income concentration is once again on the rise. Congressional Budget Office data, which include stock market returns, show 2003 was a turning point, as the only group whose share of posttax national income rose that year was the top 1 percent. For 2004, Census data reveal that average household income rose in real terms only for the top 5 percent. See Isaac Shapiro and Joel Friedman, "New CBO Data Indicate Growth in Long-Term Inequality Continues" (Washington, DC: Center on Budget and Policies Priorities, January 29, 2006), http://www.cbpp.org/1-29-06tax.htm, for more documentation of this reversal.

15. From the introduction to "The New Deal," a series by Peter Gosselin in the *Los Angeles Times*; see http://www.latimes.com/business/specials/ la-newdeal-cover,1,5066177.special?coll= la-util-nationworld-nation.

16. Jacob Hacker, "Economic Risk Has Shifted from the Government and Corporations to Workers and Their Families," *Boston Review*, September/October 2005, http://www.bostonreview.net/BR30.5/hacker.html. Hacker's book, *The Great Risk Shift* was published by Oxford University Press in 2006.

CHAPTER TWO

1. Structural deficits are deficits that expand even when we're growing at our full potential growth rate. It means our tax system is simply not calibrated correctly to bring in the revenue we're obligated to spend. The only way to fix such structural problems is to raise taxes or cut spending—you can't grow your way out of it.

2. See Jared Bernstein and Dean Baker, *The Benefits of Full Employment: When Markets Work for People* (Washington, DC: Economic Policy Institute, 2003), chap. 2, for an analysis of how this theory of an inviolable, "natural" level of unemployment has evolved over time. To be precise, the models I'm criticizing here are those conceived by the original anti-Keynesians; revisionists have tweaked the models to fit the data, but these models no longer fit the story put forth by Friedman et

al. For a pretty interesting story of the way ideology gets embedded in economics, check out the cited chapter.

3. See, for example, David Card and Alan B. Krueger, *"Myth and Measurement: The New Economics of the Minimum Wage* (Princeton, NJ: Princeton University Press, 1995).

4. Robert Moffitt, "Incentive Effects of the U.S. Welfare System: A Review," *Journal of Economic Literature* 30, no. 1 (1992):1-61.

5. Heather Boushey and Jeffrey Wenger, *Finding the Better Fit: Receiving Unemployment Insurance Increases Likelihood of Re-employment with Health Insurance*, EPI/CEPR issue brief 205 (Washington, DC: Economic Policy Institute, April 14, 2005), http://www.epinet.org/content.cfm/ib205.

6. See my debate with Stephan Moore on NPR's *Diane Rehm Show*, September 8, 2005, http://www.wamu.org/programs/dr/05/09/08.php.

7. See, I believe in incentives in these types of cases—give people an incentive to do a better job, and they often will. Punitive incentives are effective, too: my brother-in-law now wears his seatbelt because he got tired of being fined for not wearing it. For some interesting ways that incentives play out in everyday life, see the book *Freakonomics*, by Steven D. Levitt and Stephen J. Dubner (New York: William Morrow, 2005). My point is not that incentives don't matter. It's that they're no way to run an economy and they often don't have the effects their advocates claim.

8. Jacob Hacker, "The Privatization of Risk and the Increasing Economic Insecurity of Americans," an article on the Web site of the Social Science Research Council, October 24, 2005, http://privatizationofrisk.ssrc.org/Hacker/.

9. In fact, that's a central theme of moving from a YOYO back to a WITT society: evening out the distribution of wealth, health, education, opportunity, and so on. The idea is to use the collective will of the people and the power of the government to distribute risks and resources in such a way as to ensure that individuals can pursue their potential.

10. For an excellent analysis of these points, see Rob Atkinson, *Supply-Side*

Follies: How Conservative Economics Threatens Innovation and Prosperity, and What Progressives Should Do about It (Lanham, MD: Rowman and Littlefield, forthcoming, 2006).

11. John Maynard Keynes, *The General Theory of Employment, Interest, and Money* (New York: First Harvest/Harcourt, 1964), 383.

12. Sylvia Allegretto, *Basic Family Budgets*, briefing paper 165 (Washington, DC: Economic Policy Institute, September 2005), http://www.epi.org/content.cfm/bp165.

13. Jared Bernstein, "Wages Picture," an article on the Web site of the Economic Policy Institute, October 28, 2005, http://www.epi.org/content.cfm/webfeat_econindicators_wages_20051028.

14. Quoted in Jonathan Weisman, "Snow Concedes Economic Surge Is Not Benefiting People Equally," *Washington Post*, sec. A, August 9, 2005.

15. John Edwards, a WITT advocate throughout his political career, has crafted a plan in this spirit called "College for Everyone," which provides free first-year tuition to a community college or state university for every qualified student willing to work part time.

CHAPTER THREE

1. Months later, the negative publicity around this "bridge to nowhere" led Congress to force the senator, Ted Stevens of Alaska, to strike the project, but he got to keep the money, presumably for some other transportation project.

2. Hendrik Hertzberg, "Abramoffed," *New Yorker*, January 16, 2006, http://www.newyorker.com/talk/content/articles/060116ta_talk_hertzberg.

3. U.S. Congressional Budget Office, *The Long-Term Budget Outlook* (Washington, DC: December 2005), http://www.cbo.gov/ftpdocs/69xx/doc6982/12-15-LongTermOutlook.pdf.

4. Scott Liell, *46 Pages: Thomas Paine, Common Sense, and the Turning Point to Independence* (Philadelphia: Running Press, 2003).

5. The brains behind this operation belonged to Ruth Sando of Sando Associates. My colleague Sylvia Allegretto of the Economic Policy Institute also helped to run the groups.

6. A related problem is that as non-college-educated workers leave the dwindling manufacturing sector, they add to the labor supply of the lower end of the service sector, creating downward pressure of wage growth. It's also the case that wage inequality is significantly greater in services than in manufacturing, so this employment shift is also associated with faster-growing inequality.

7. Alan Blinder, "Equality and Security," statement to the Democratic Forum on the Economy, September 23, 2005, http://jec.senate.gov/democrats/Documents/Hearings/blindertestimony23sep2005.pdf.

8. Lawrence Mishel, Jared Bernstein, and Sylvia Allegretto, *The State of Working America, 2004-05* (Ithaca, NY: Cornell University Press, 2005).

9. Cited in Felix G. Rohatyn and Warren Rudman, "It's Time to Rebuild America," *Washington Post*, sec. A, December 13, 2005.

10. Drew Altman, president of the Kaiser Family Foundation, quoted in Peter Gosselin, "Health Plan to Revive Debate," *Los Angeles Times*, January 23, 2006, http://www.latimes.com/news/politics/la-na-health23jan23,0,1934133,full.story?coll=la-headlines-politics.

11. Ben Bernanke, "The Outlook for the Economy and for Policy," statement to the National Association for Business Economics, September 27, 2005, http://www.whitehouse.gov/cea/econ-outlook20050927.pdf.

12. Paul Krugman, "One Nation, Uninsured," *New York Times*, sec. A, June 13, 2005.

13. Author's analysis of 2004 data for persons under 65 (to avoid confounding the analysis with Medicare coverage, which is virtually universal for the elderly — and is the very nonmarket solution I'm advocating).

14. Steve Savner and Jared Bernstein, "Can Better Skills Meet Better Jobs?" *The American Prospect*, September 1, 2004, http://www.prospect.org/web/page.ww?section=root&name=ViewPrint&articleId=8357.

15. See, for example, David Lee, "Inequality in the United States during the 1980s: Rising Dispersion or Falling Minimum Wage? *Quarterly Journal of Economics* 114, no. 3 (1999):977–1023.

16. Many have, and one of the great ones is Carnoy et al., *The Charter School Dust-Up*, the best evaluation of charter school outcomes thus far. For a WITT-style solution, see Rick Kahlenberg's book, which shares not only a similar sensibility to this book but also a similar title: *All Together Now: Creating Middle-Class Schools through Public School Choice*. (He thought of it first, though I had forgotten it, at least consciously, when I began writing this book.) Finally, in *Class Matters*, Richard Rothstein takes a close, commonsense look at the impact of class on education outcomes, shining bright light on the disadvantages that low-income children bring with them to school.

17. Kahlenberg, *All Together Now*.

CHAPTER FOUR

1. Mishel, Bernstein, and Allegretto, *State of Working America*, 62, table 1.10.

2. See Gary Langer, "Health Care Pains: Growing Health Care Concerns Fuel Cautious Support for Change," an analysis of the poll results on the ABC News Web site, http://abcnews.go.com/sections/living/ US/healthcare031020_poll.html.

3. These poll results can be seen at http://online.wsj.com/public/article/SB112973460667273222-7Jjp4Ckx_LsV4qI5rjzrENNIcAQ_20061020.html?mod=blogs.

4. Poll results can be found on "Analyze the Issues and Coalitions," a page on *Beyond Red vs. Blue: The 2005 Political Typology*, the Web site of the Pew Research Center for the People and the Press, http://typology.people-press.org/data/index.php?QuestionID=26.

5. Ibid., http://typology.people-press.org/data/index.php?QuestionID=25.

6. Jared Bernstein, "It's Still the Economy, Stupid: Six Reasons Why This Election *Didn't* Discredit Pocketbook Campaigning," *The American Prospect*, November 15, 2004, http://www.prospect.org/web/page.ww?section=root&name=ViewWeb&articleId=8852.

7. See an interesting paper by Larry Bartels, "What's the Matter with *What's the Matter with Kansas?*" (prepared for presentation at the annual meeting of the American Political Science Association, Washington, DC, September 1-4, 2005), http://www.princeton.edu/~bartels/kansas.pdf.

8. See David Broder, "For Democrats, a Path Back to Power," *Washington Post*, sec. A, October 13, 2005, http://www.washingtonpost.com/wp-dyn/content/article/2005/10/12/AR2005101202000.html.

9. Liell, *46 Pages*, 18.

10. Ibid., 17.

11. I thank my EPI colleague Max Sawicky for these numbers.

12. See the analysis of costs by Amy Belasco, *The Cost of Iraq, Afghanistan and Enhanced Base Security Since 9/11* (Washington, DC: Congressional Research Service, October 7, 2005), http://www.fas.org/sgp/crs/natsec/RL33110.pdf.

13. Bruce Bartlett, statement to the Democratic Forum on the Economy, September 23, 2005, http://democrats.senate.gov/dpc/forums/forum01/bartlett.pdf.

14. George Packer, "Talk of the Town: Game Plan," *The New Yorker*, October 24, 2005, 31, http://www.newyorker.com/talk/content/articles/051024ta_talk_packer.

15. See Lawrence Korb, *The Korb Report: A Realistic Defense for America* (New York: Business Leaders for Sensible Priorities, n.d.), http://www.sensiblepriorities.org/pdf/korb_report_Finalb.pdf.

16. For the record, the federal budget by no means needs to always be in balance. In fact, to enforce such a rule is harmful, because deficit spending, especially Keynesian stimulus, is often warranted in hard times and in periods when we need to ratchet up productivity-enhancing public investments. The key is to avoid situations like the current one, where the debt-to-GDP ratio just keeps growing. That's the unsustainable part.

CONCLUSION

1. The speech can be found at http://www.knox.edu/x9803.xml.

2. "Remarks of Tom Vilsack to the 2005 DLC National Conversation," July 26, 2005, http://www.dlc.org/ndol_ci.cfm?kaid=137&subid=900109&contentid=253480.

3. Tom Vilsack, "Ideology of Contempt," *Blueprint Magazine*, October 21, 2005, http://www.dlc.org/ndol_ci.cfm?kaid=137&subid=900109&contentid=253589.

4. Here's a speech by Edwards that's steeped in the WITT agenda and mind-set: "The America We Believe In," *TomPaine.com*, January 31, 2006, http://www.tompaine.com/articles/20060131/the_america_we_believe_in.php.

APPENDIX

1. Lee Price, *The Boom That Wasn't: The Economy Has Little to Show for $860 Billion in Tax Cuts*, briefing paper 168 (Washington, DC: Economic Policy Institute, 2005).

2. See, for example, the Congressional Budget Office's forecast of the effects of the Bush tax cuts on the economy, "How CBO Analyzed the Macroeconomic Effects of the President's Budget," July 2003, http://www.cbo.gov/showdoc.cfm?index=4454&sequence=0. This analysis is particularly germane because the CBO attempted to model the very supply-side effects that YOYOs argued were engendered by the Bush tax cuts. The result: the tax cuts would be as likely to slightly lower growth as to slightly raise it. Most damning, when the CBO tried to isolate the impact of just the supply-side claims (the YOYO notion that cutting taxes would encourage greater investment and more jobs), the models showed uniformly negative results: slower growth and bigger deficits.

INDEX

A

ACORN (Association for Community Organization and Reform Now), 126
Afghanistan war, 104, 115
African Americans poverty rates, 89
Alaska bridge project, 61–62, 104, 139
All Together Now agenda. *See also* WITT.
  education policies, 93
  first step, 40, 71
  framing solutions, 71
  globalization
    Apollo Alliance, 76
    demand replacement, 75–76
    direct job creation, 75–76
    earnings of workers, 73
    energy independence, 75–76
    hourly workers, 73
    manufacturing sector jobs, 72–76
    offshoring white collar jobs, 73–74
    problem statement, 72–74
    safety nets for workers, 75
    Trade Administration Assistance, 75
    trade imbalance, 73
    WITT solution, 74–76
  health care
    administrative costs, 80
    as a commodity, 82
    costs, *versus* other countries, 77
    Medicare for All, 79–81
    Medicare fraud, 81–82
    Medicare savings, 80
    per capita costs, 77
    pooling risk, 78
    prescription drug plan, 82–84
    problem statement, 77–78
    public support for Medicare, 79–80
    rationing, 80
    WITT solution, 78–84
  income inequality
    1995 – 2000, 88–89
    bargaining power, 87–88
    compensation *versus* productivity, 84–86, 87
    direct job creation, 91
    Employee Free Choice Act, 91
    full employment, 87
    Full Employment and Balanced Growth Act of 1978, 90

    hourly compensation, 85
    Humphrey-Hawkins Act, 90
    living-standard slippage, 86
    median family incomes, 89
    minimum wages, 91
    poverty rates, 89
    problem statement, 84–87
    real income losses, 86
    role of the Federal Reserve, 89–90
    stock holdings, 85
    top *versus* bottom, 84
    unemployment rates, 89–90
    unions, 88, 91
    WITT solution, 87–92
    working more to compensate, 86
  planks in the platform, 92–94
Allbaugh, Joe, 14
anti-monopoly regulations, 31–32
Apollo Alliance, globalization, 76
Association for Community Organization and Reform Now (ACORN), 126

B

Baker, Dean, 88
bargaining power
  in a "buyer's market," 97–98
  collective bargaining rights, 43
  income inequality, 87–88
Bartlett, Bruce, 104
Bernanke, Ben, 78
Blair, Tony, 117–118
Blinder, Alan, 73–74
Brandeis, Louis, 30, 41
Brooks, David, 15
Brown, Gordon, 118
Bush, George. H. W., government spending, 103
Bush, George W.
  anti-good-government, 104
  deficit growth, 52–53
  government spending, 103–105
  Ownership Society, 5
  prescription drug plan, 82–84
  prevailing wage rule, 8
  productivity growth, 134
  spending, 63–64
  spending as share of the economy, 63–64

C

capital gains, tax cuts, 35, 112
Carnegie, Andrew, 30
Carter, Jimmy, 46–47
Cheney, Dick, 66–67
child care costs, 56
child-support enforcement, spending cuts, 35
class biases, in economic policy, 40
Clinton, Hillary, 102
Clinton, William, 103, 133
collective bargaining rights, 43
College for Everyone, 139
Common Sense, 9–10
compensation. *See* family income; income inequality; real income; wages.
concentration of wealth, 30–31, 137. *See also* redistribution of wealth.
confidence in government, 61
Coolidge, Calvin, 30

D

Davis-Bacon Act of 1931, 44
debt. *See* deficits; spending, government.
defense spending
    antiquated weapons, 115
    budget, 115
    wars in Iraq and Afghanistan, 104, 115
deficits. *See also* spending, government.
    under Bush, G. W., 52–53
    Cheney's views on, 66–67
    decimation of revenue base, 65
    effects of, 65
    freezing discretionary programs, 65
    role of the electorate, 66–67
    spending cuts, 66
    structural, 137
Democrats
    fear of populism, 108–109
    perceived lack of success, 106–107
    versus Republicans
        economic policies, 107
        federal spending, 64
        full employment, 55
        globalization, 107
        YOYO policies, 54–55
    senior citizens, views of, 60–62
    YOYO policies, 54–55, 60
    YOYO political strategy, 108
Depression era. *See* Great Depression.
deregulation, effects of
    economic outcomes, 32
    employment, 32
    GDP (gross domestic product), 32

government as a whore, 63
    investment, 32
    productivity, 32
Dionne, E. J., 106
dividend income, tax cuts, 35, 112

E

EARN (Economic Analysis and Research Network), 126
Earned Income Tax Credit, 52
economic growth, *versus* personal, 57–58
economic outcomes
    deregulation, effects of, 32
    employment, 32
    GDP (gross domestic product), 32
    investment, 32
    productivity, 32
    tax cuts, 32
    YOYO policies, 32, 131–134
economic policy. *See also* WITT; YOYO.
    goals of, 39–40
    history of. *See* history of economic and social policy.
    inherent class biases, 40
economists
    Bartlett, Bruce, 104
    Bernanke, Ben, 78
    Blinder, Alan, 73–74
    Friedman, Milton, 46–47
    Keynes, John Maynard, 41–47, 54
    Lucas, Robert, 47
    Mishel, Lawrence, 73
    Price, Lee, 134
    Shiller, Robert, 21–22
education
    college
        College for Everyone, 139
        public sentiment, 103
        student aid, spending cuts, 35, 39
        universal access to, 59
    job training
        blaming the victim, 108
        as global solution, 55–59
        hyper-individualism, 59
        inadequacy of, 108
        personal responsibility, 59
        spending cuts, 35, 39
    public
        charter school outcomes, 141
        disadvantages of low-income children, 141
        impact of class on, 141
        integration by income level, 93–94
        WITT policies, 93

Edwards, John, 127–128, 139
Eisenberry, Ross, 98
electorate
    effects of YOYOism, 95–96
    role in deficits, 66–67
    single-issue voters, 101–103
    support for conservatives, 99
    voting against economic interests,
        99–101
    on WITT *versus* YOYO, 70–71
Employee Free Choice Act, 91
employment. *See also* unemployment.
    among the poor, 49
    bargaining power
        in a "buyer's market," 97–98
        collective bargaining rights, 43
        income inequality, 87–88
    "buyer's market," 97–98
    demand replacement, 75–76
    deregulation, effects of, 32
    direct job creation, 75–76, 91
    economic outcome of YOYO
        policies, 32
    full
        benefits of, 87–88
        definition, 87
        Democrats *versus* Republicans, 55
        effects of, 44–45
        funding, 113
        Humphrey-Hawkins Act, 90
        income inequality, 87
        Keynes' views on, 44
        last period of, 88–89
        policy shift away from, 20
    growth rate, 32
    overtime regulation, 43, 98
    privatization, effects of, 32
    rates, and hyper-individualism, 59
    security trends, 34
    supply-side economics, 53, 133–134
    tax cuts, effects of, 32
energy independence, globalization, 75–76

F

"faith based organizations," 14
family income. *See also* income inequality;
    real income; wages.
    census data, 137
    child care costs, 56
    decline in, 56
    economic growth, *versus* personal,
        57–58
    health care costs, 56
    housing costs, 56

income inequality, 89
    jobless recovery, 58
    median, 57–58
    post-WWII, 6
    and productivity, 6, 57–58
    real income, historical growth, 32
    rise in, 137
    since the mid-1970s, 6
    supply-side economics, 133–134
    volatility, causes of, 34–35
    vulnerability to economic shifts, 34
    working more hours, 57–58
    and YOYO policies, 6–7
Federal Reserve Bank, 41, 89–90
FEMA (Federal Emergency Management),
    13–15
food stamps, spending cuts, 35, 39
Friedman, Milton, 46–47
full employment
    benefits of, 87–88
    definition, 87
    Democrats *versus* Republicans, 55
    funding, 113
    Humphrey-Hawkins Act, 90
    income inequality, 87
    Keynes' views on, 44
    last period of, 88–89
    policy shift away from, 20
Full Employment and Balanced Growth
    Act of 1978, 90

G

gap between rich and poor, 31–32
GDP (gross domestic product)
    deregulation, effects of, 32
    economic outcome of YOYO policies,
        32
    government spending and revenues,
        63–64
    growth rate, 32
    history of economic and social policy,
        32
    privatization, effects of, 32
    tax cuts, effects of, 32
Gladwell, Malcolm, 24
globalization
    blaming the victim, 108
    WITT agenda
        Apollo Alliance, 76
        demand replacement, 75–76
        direct job creation, 75–76
        earnings of workers, 73
        energy independence, 75–76
        hourly workers, 73

manufacturing sector jobs, 72–76
offshoring white collar jobs, 73–74
problem statement, 72–74
safety nets for workers, 75
Trade Administration Assistance, 75
trade imbalance, 73
WITT solution, 74–76
WITT movement, 128
Gosselin, Peter, 14, 34, 106
government
collaborative solutions, 68–71
confidence in, 61
getting off our backs, 46–47
incompetence, poll results, 101
middle-income familys' view of, 69–71
Paine's views on, 67–71
revenue. See revenue, government.
role for regulation, 69–70
spending. See spending, government.
as a whore, 63
Great Depression. See also stock market, crash of 1929.
collective bargaining rights, 43
economic risk management, 33
minimum wage, 43
public works projects, 43
Social Security, 43
unemployment insurance, 43
unemployment rate, 41
unemployment rates, 41
Greenspan, Alan, 38–39, 89–90
gross domestic product (GDP). See GDP (gross domestic product).

H

Hacker, Jacob, 34, 106
health care. See also HSAs (Health Savings Accounts); Medicaid; Medicare; Medicare for All.
cost to employers, 113
cost to families, 56
government provided, efficiency of, 115
Japanese, 113
less government, 27–28
market solutions, 28–29
versus other countries, 51–52
polls, 97, 101
prescription drug plan, 82–84, 103–104
rationing, 51–52
trends, 34
uninsured, number of, 5, 51
WITT agenda
administrative costs, 80
as a commodity, 82

costs, versus other countries, 77
Medicare for All, 79–81
Medicare fraud, 81–82
Medicare savings, 80
per capita costs, 77
pooling risk, 78
prescription drug plan, 82–84
problem statement, 77–78
public support for Medicare, 79–80
rationing, 80
WITT solution, 78–84
Health Savings Accounts (HSAs). See HSAs (Health Savings Accounts).
Hertzberg, Hendrik, 63
Hispanic poverty rates, 89
history of economic and social policy
1920s, 30, 41
1920s versus 1980s, 31–32
1930s, 43
1970s, 46–47
anti-monopoly regulations, 31–32
concentration of wealth, 30–31
deregulation, economic outcomes, 32
economic risk shift, 32–33
employment growth, 32
Federal Reserve Bank, 41
gap between rich and poor, 31–32
GDP (gross domestic product), 32
Great Depression
collective bargaining rights, 43
economic risk management, 33
minimum wage, 43
public works projects, 43
Social Security, 43
unemployment insurance, 43
unemployment rates, 41
and WITT philosophy, 45
incentive-based economics, 46–47
investment growth, 32
"invisible hand" of the free market, 30, 42–43, 46
Keynesian economics, 41–47
monetarism, 47
neoclassical economics, 47
peaks and valleys of inequality, 30–31
periods of inequality, 31–32
privatization, economic outcomes, 32
productivity growth, 32
rational expectations, 47
real income growth, 32
redistribution of wealth, 32
risk sharing, 43
stagflation, 46
stock market crash of 1929, 41
tax cuts, economic outcomes, 32

unemployment rates, 41
WITT arrival, 43–45
hourly workers, 73, 85
housing costs, 56
HSAs (Health Savings Accounts). *See also*
health care.
comparative shopping, 25
corporate solutions, 26
cost drivers, 25
description, 24–25
resource sharing, 26–27
risk sharing, 26–27
shrinking the role of government, 26
versus Social Security privatization,
25–27
Humphrey-Hawkins Act, 90
Hurricane Katrina. *See* Katrina.
hyper-individualism
barrier to WITT policies, 54
concentration of resources, 45
definition, 4
education and jobs training, 59
employment rates, 59
health care. *See* HSAs (Health Savings
Accounts).
moral hazard, 27–28
pooling risks, 27
role in current problems, 10–11
Social Security, 20–24
starving the beast, 15
unintended consequences, 50–54

I

IAF (Industrial Area Foundation), 126
incentive-based economics, 46–47, 138
income. *See* family income; income
inequality; real income; wages.
income inequality. *See also* family income;
real income; wages.
historical periods of, 31–32
peaks and valleys of, 30–31
WITT agenda. *See also* family
income.
1995 - 2000, 88–89
bargaining power, 87–88
compensation *versus* productivity,
84–86, 87
direct job creation, 91
Employee Free Choice Act, 91
full employment, 87
Full Employment and Balanced
Growth Act of 1978, 90
hourly compensation, 85
Humphrey-Hawkins Act, 90

living-standard slippage, 86
median family incomes, 89
minimum wages, 91
poverty rates, 89
problem statement, 84–87
real income losses, 86
role of the Federal Reserve, 89–90
stock holdings, 85
top *versus* bottom, 84
unemployment rates, 89–90
unions, 88, 91
WITT solution, 87–92
working more to compensate, 86
individual Social Security accounts. *See*
Social Security, privatization.
individualism, excessive. *See* hyper-individualism.
Industrial Area Foundation (IAF), 126
interventionism
Keynesian economics, 42–43
Reagan era, 47
unintended consequences, 52–54
WITT policies, 75
YOYO reactions to, 55–56
investment
deregulation, effects of, 32
economic outcome of YOYO
policies, 32
growth rate, 32
privatization, effects of, 32
supply-side economics, 53, 133–134
tax cuts, effects of, 32
"invisible hand" of the free market, 30,
42–43, 46
Iraq war, 104, 115

J

Japanese health care, 113
job training. *See* education, job training.
jobless recovery, 6, 58
jobs. *See* employment; unemployment.

K

Kahlenberg, Richard, 93
Kansas, voting against economic interests,
99–101
Katrina
cleanup costs, 14
government response to, 13–15
lessons from, 124–125
opportunity for change, 16–18
post-storm analysis, 16–18
prevailing wage rule, 8

recovery costs, 14, 16, 104
role of government, 14–15
"starve the beast" mentality, 15
Keynes, John Maynard, 41–47, 54
Keynesian economics, 41–47
Korb, Lawrence, 115
Krugman, Paul, 14–15, 79–80, 106
Kucinich, Dennis, 113

L

LaGuardia, Fiorella, 111
leadership, quality of, 10
Liell, Scott, 67, 102
living-standard slippage, 86
Lucas, Robert, 47

M

manufacturing sector, globalization, 72–76,
140
mealtime in heaven and hell, 3
median family income, 57–58
Medicaid, spending cuts, 35, 39
Medicare
expansion costs, 103–104
fraud, 81–82
polls, 97
public support for, 79–80
savings, 80
universal. See Medicare for All.
Medicare for All
benefits of, 79–81
funding, 113–114
polls, 96–97
rationing, 81
minimum wage
All Together Now agenda, 91
effects of, 48
Fair Labor Standards Act, 97–98
Great Depression, 43
history of, 43
income inequality, 91
polls, 98, 101
public support for, 98, 101
Reagan era, 91–92
trends, 92
WITT agenda, 91
Mishel, Lawrence, 73
monetarism, 47
moral hazard
definition, 27
unemployment, 28
YOYO policies, 48
moral values, 102

N

"natural" levels of unemployment, 137–138
"natural rights," 10
neoclassical economics, 47
New Orleans, hurricane. See Katrina.

O

Obama, Barack, 123
offshoring white collar jobs, 73–74. See also
globalization.
"opportunity society," 101
overtime regulation
Fair Labor Standards Act, 98
polls, 101
time-and-a-half suspended, 43
Ownership Society, 5, 123–124

P

Packer, George, 104
Paine, Thomas
". . . begin the world over again.", 127
influence on WITT, 67–71
on "natural rights," 10
parallels to modern times, 9–10
on results of current action, 129
on type of government, 67–71
on uniting a populace, 102–103
pensions. See also retirement; Social
Security.
defined contribution plans, 35
market solutions, 28–29
trends, 34
United Airlines, 69
Personal Reemployment Accounts (PRAs),
27–28
personal responsibility
education and jobs training, 59
health care. See HSAs (Health Savings
Accounts).
Social Security. See HSAs (Health Savings Accounts); Social Security, privatization.
unemployment. See PRAs (Personal
Reemployment Accounts).
polls
confidence in government, 61
Democrats lack of success, 106–107
government incompetence, 101
health care, 97, 101
Medicare for All, 96–97
minimum wage, 98, 101
moral values, 102
overtime regulation, 101

satisfaction with leadership, 122–123
Social Security privatization, 97, 101
populism, fear of, 108–109
poverty
    African Americans, 89
    children, in the United Kingdom,
      117–118
    Hispanics, 89
    income inequality, 89
    Reagan era, 53
    trends, 2000 - 2004, 53
PRAs (Personal Reemployment Accounts),
    27–28
prescription drug plan, 82–84, 103–104
prevailing wage rule, 8, 44
Price, Lee, 134
privatization
    economic outcomes, 32
    effects of
      employment, 32
      gross domestic product, 32
      investment, 32
      productivity, 32
    effects on GDP (gross domestic prod-
      uct), 32
    Social Security. *See* Social Security,
      privatization.
productivity
    under Bush (G. W.), 134
    versus compensation, 84–86, 87
    deregulation, effects of, 32
    economic outcome of YOYO policies,
      32
    and family income, 6, 57–58, 73
    growth rate, 32
    historical growth, 32
    versus individual growth, 6
    privatization, effects of, 32
    and real wages, 120
    tax cuts, effects of, 32
public education. *See* education, public.
public opinion. *See* polls.
public works projects, history of, 43

Q

Quarles, Randal K., 58–59

R

rational expectations, 47
rationing health care, 51–52, 80
Reagan, Ronald
    boom era, 133
    getting government off our backs, 46–47

government spending, 103
    interventionism, 47
    minimum wages, 91–92
    poverty rates, 53
    real income trends, 53
    supply-side economics, 52, 53, 133
real income. *See also* family income;
    income inequality; wages.
    1979 - 2000, 96
    1999 - 2004, 120
    historical growth, 32
    by income level, 96
    losses, 86
    productivity and, 120
    tax cuts and, 96
    trends, Reagan era, 53
redistribution of wealth, 32, 53. *See also*
    concentration of wealth.
reforming economic policy. *See* All
    Together Now agenda; WITT.
Republicans
    versus Democrats
      economic policies, 107
      federal spending, 64
      full employment, 55
      globalization, 107
      YOYO policies, 54–55
      fiscal integrity, 104
retirement, less government, 27–28. *See
    also* pensions; Social Security.
revenue, government
    deficits, and the revenue base, 65
    and the gross domestic product, 63–64
    as share of economy, 63–64
    supply-side economics, 53
risks
    avoidance. *See* moral hazard.
    pooling, 27
    sharing
      history of, 43
      HSAs, 26–27
      Social Security privatization, 23
    shifting
      history of, 32–33
      history of economic and social pol-
        icy, 32–33
      from large bodies to individuals,
        33–36
      YOYO goals, 4
Rockefeller, John D., 30
Roosevelt, Theodore, 30
Roosevelt Institution, 126–127

S

safety nets for workers, 75
Savner, Steve, 90–91
service sector *versus* manufacturing, 140
Shiller, Robert, 21–22
single-issue voters, 101–103
Snow, John, 58, 89
Social Darwinism, 123–124
social policy, history of. *See* history of economic and social policy.
Social Security. *See also* pensions; retirement.
    administrative costs, 51
    elderly poverty rate, 51
    history of, 43
    hyper-individualism, 20–24
    number of recipients, 51
    privatization
      aged *versus* working-age population, 21
      Bush's role in, 18–20
      costs (2004), 20
      cycle of capital, 21
      description, 18
      government bond investment, 22
      versus health care costs, 20
      versus HSAs, 25–27
      income test, 19
      individual accounts, 21, 135
      investment security, 21–22
      means test, 19
      objectives, real, 20–24
      objectives, stated, 19–20
      outliving benefits, 22
      paying existing recipients, 135
      polls, 97, 101
      predicted solvency, 19
      risk sharing, 23
      stock market cycles and retirement income, 22
      stock market investment, 21–22, 136
    role in income for the elderly, 20, 51
spending, government. *See also* deficits; starving the beast.
    Bush, George. H. W., 103
    Bush, George W., 63–64, 103–105
    Clinton, William, 103
    cuts
      child-support enforcement, 35
      college aid, 39
      education and jobs training, 35, 39
      food stamps, 35, 39
      Medicaid, 35, 39
      in response to deficits, 66
      student aid, 35
    defense budget, 115
    Katrina recovery, 14, 16, 104
    Medicare expansion, 103–104
    per capita, 64
    percent of U. S. economy, 64
    prescription drug plan, 103–104
    under Reagan, 103
    as share of the economy, 63–64
    total, 64
    transportation bill, 61, 104
    wars in Iraq and Afghanistan, 104, 115
    YOYO policies, 103–105
stagflation, 46
starving the beast. *See also* spending, government.
    definition, 4
    hyper-individualism, 15
    living off debt, 53
Stevens, Ted, 139
stock holdings, 85
stock market
    crash of 1929, 41. *See also* Great Depression.
    failures, 29
    investment security, 21–22
    Social Security investment, 136
    technology bubble, 136–137
student aid, spending cuts, 35
supply-side economics
    employment, 53, 133–134
    family income, 133–134
    investment, 53, 133–134
    Reagan era, 52, 53, 133
    revenue, government, 53
    tax cuts, 143
    trickle-down theory, 133–134

T

tax cuts
    capital gains, 35, 112
    dividend income, 35, 112
    economic outcomes, 32
    effects of
      Congressional Budget Office forecast, 143
      economic outcomes, 32
      employment, 32
      gross domestic product, 32
      investment, 32
      Katrina recovery, 50
      productivity, 32
      unintended consequences, 53
    estate taxes, 35

expiration, 111
Greenspan's influence, 38–39
and real income, 96
sunsetting, 111
supply-side economics, 143
time-and-a-half for overtime. *See* overtime
regulation.
Trade Administration Assistance, 75
trade imbalance, 73
transportation bill, 61, 104, 139
trickle-down theory, 133–134

U

U. S. economy, dollar figures, 64
unemployment. *See also* employment.
insurance, 43, 49–50
jobless recovery, 6
less government, 27–28
market solutions, 28–29
"natural" levels, 137–138
personal responsibility, 28. *See also*
PRAs (Personal Reemployment
Accounts).
PRAs (Personal Reemployment
Accounts), 27–28
rate
current, 41
Great depression, 41
income inequality, 89–90
YOYO policies, *versus* WITT, 45
uninsured, health care, 5, 51
unintended consequences
hyper-individualism, 50–54
interventionism, 52–54
tax cuts, 53
WITT, 49
YOYO policies, 50–54
unions
declining membership, 91
goals of, 88
income inequality, 88, 91
waning power, 88
United Airlines bankruptcy, 69
United Kingdom, child poverty, 117–118

V

Vilsack, Tom, 9, 124
voters. *See* electorate.
voting against economic interests, 99–101

W

wages. *See also* family income; income
inequality; real income.
effects of globalization, 73
minimum wage, 43, 48
versus productivity, 84–86, 87
time-and-a-half for overtime, 43
war on terror, 110–111, 115
wars in Afghanistan and Iraq, 104, 115
welfare
benefits, effects of, 48–49
Earned Income Tax Credit, 52
reform, effects of, 52
reform act, 49
WITT (We're in this together). *See also* All
Together Now agenda.
agenda
college, universal access to, 59
cost of, 50–54, 111–115
fear of populism, 108–109
funding, 112–115
healing our divisions, 95–102
health care. *See* All Together Now
agenda, health care; HSAs
(Health Savings Accounts); Medicaid; Medicare; Medicare for All.
income inequality, services *versus*
manufacturing, 140
pervasiveness of the YOYO ethos,
107–108
winning support for, 106–115
benefits of, 50–54
core beliefs, 8
description, 7–9
evolution of, 17
movement
globalization, 128
historic victories, 126
leadership, 122–127
the message, 120–122
the messengers, 122–127
public conversation about, 119–120
supportive organizations, 126–127
optimism of, 101–103
unintended consequences, 49

Y

YOYO (You're on your own)
assumptions, 37–38, 47–50
benefits of, 50–54
core competence, 110–111
costs of, 50–54
definition, 4

Democrats *versus* Republicans, 54–55
economic outcome, 32, 131–134
education policies, 93
evolution of, 34–36
fiscal conservatism, 103–105
and foreign policy, 110
goals, 4

interventionism, 55
myths, 47–50
pessimism of, 101–103
rules for government, 48
scientific basis for, 37–38
unintended consequences, 50–54

JARED BERNSTEIN joined the Economic Policy Institute in 1992, where he directs EPI's research on living standards. He is a widely published author in both the popular press and academic journals and is the coauthor of seven editions of the book *The State of Working America*. Mr. Bernstein is a frequent media commentator on a broad range of economic issues. He holds a Ph.D. in social welfare from Columbia University.

About Berrett-Koehler Publishers

Berrett–Koehler is an independent publisher dedicated to an ambitious mission: Creating a World that Works for All.

We believe that to truly create a better world, action is needed at all levels — individual, organizational, and societal. At the individual level, our publications help people align their lives and work with their deepest values. At the organizational level, our publications promote progressive leadership and management practices, socially responsible approaches to business, and humane and effective organizations. At the societal level, our publications advance social and economic justice, shared prosperity, sustainable development, and new solutions to national and global issues.

A major theme of our publications is "Opening Up New Space." They challenge conventional thinking, introduce new points of view, and offer new alternatives for change. Their common quest is changing the underlying beliefs, mindsets, institutions, and structures that keep generating the same cycles of problems, no matter who our leaders are or what improvement programs we adopt.

We strive to practice what we preach—to operate our publishing company in line with the ideas in our books. At the core of our approach is stewardship, which we define as a deep sense of responsibility to administer the company for the benefit of all of our "stakeholder" groups: authors, customers, employees, investors, service providers, and the communities and environment around us. We seek to establish a partnering relationship with each stakeholder that is open, equitable, and collaborative.

We are gratified that thousands of readers, authors, and other friends of the company consider themselves to be part of the "BK Community." We hope that you, too, will join our community and connect with us through the ways described on our website at www.bkconnection.com.

A BK Currents Title

This book is part of our BK Currents series. BK Currents titles advance social and economic justice by exploring the critical intersections between business and society. Offering a unique combination of thoughtful analysis and progressive alternatives, BK Currents titles promote positive change at the national and global levels. To find out more, visit www.bkcurrents.com.

BE CONNECTED

Visit Our Website

Go to www.bkconnection.com to read exclusive previews and ex-
cerpts of new books, find detailed information on all Berrett-Koehler
titles and authors, browse subject-area libraries of books, and get special discounts.

Subscribe to Our Free E-Newsletter

Be the first to hear about new publications, special discount offers,
exclusive articles, news about bestsellers, and more! Get on the list for
our free e-newsletter by going to www.bkconnection.com.

Participate in the Discussion

To see what others are saying about our books and post your own
thoughts, check out our blogs at www.bkblogs.com.

Get Quantity Discounts

Berrett-Koehler books are available at quantity discounts for orders of
ten or more copies. Please call us toll-free at (800) 929-2929 or email us
at bkp.orders@aidcvt.com.

Host a Reading Group

For tips on how to form and carry on a book reading group in your workplace or community, see our website at www.bkconnection.com.

Join the BK Community

Thousands of readers of our books have become part of the "BK Community" by participating in events featuring our authors, reviewing
draft manuscripts of forthcoming books, spreading the word about
their favorite books, and supporting our publishing program in other
ways. If you would like to join the BK Community, please contact us
at bkcommunity@bkpub.com.